Content Creation and Promotion Explained!

Steven Christianson

Copyright © 2021 Steven Christianson

Content Creation and Promotion – Explained!

by Steven Christianson.
Published by Amazon *KDP*

All rights reserved. No portion of this book may be reproduced in any form without permission from the publisher, except as permitted by copyright law in Canada and the United States. For permissions contact: stevenchristianson.ca

Cover design by Josée Scalabrini and Henley Point Productions

ISBN-13: 979-8-5905-0914-0

To the girls who make every moment worthwhile.

CONTENTS

	Interview with the Author	iv
	Acknowledgments	vii
	Part 1 – Foundations	1
1	Looking Around	5
2	It's an Illusion	15
3	Savour the Problem to Achieve Authority and Influence	25
	Part 2 – Considerations	31
4	Social Causes and Issues	35
5	Corporate Social Positioning	45
6	What's in a Name?	55
	Part 3 – Perspectives	63
7	The Importance of People: Lessons from a Circus Man	67
8	Pros and Cons of Visual Identifiers	75
9	Music as a Promotional Tool	85
10	Soundmarks and Audio Logos	95
	Part 4 – Essentials	101
11	Social Commerce	105
12	Trust and Authority	115

13	Putting Persuasion into Action	125
14	How Do We Know We're Going in The Right Direction?	153
15	Ultimately, …	163
16	Looking Ahead	171
	Take-Aways, Questions and Answers	178
	Social Media Take-Aways	182
	Glossary	212
	Further Reading	216
	Index	220
	About *Explained!*	223
	Coming Soon - *Podcasting*	226
	About the Author	228

Interview with the Author

What inspired this book?

It was really two things. First, I'm always inspired by innovation, and the creative innovativeness in social platforms like *Anchor* really lit a spark. I had been hosting my newest podcast for about a year, and began thinking about sharing that and similar content in a complementary medium. The second spark originates in much of the work I do in government and public relations. Those experiences and interactions with a variety of people have created a repository of fodder in my head; again, something I thought was suitable for sharing.

What is content creation?

Today, content is what you put out there. It can be a product or service. The blog you write, the storyline and footage of your film, the podcast you host, the video you create and upload – this is all content. Essentially, it is anything that is directed toward an end-user, market segment or audience.

Is this new, and the result of social media?

Content creation and promotion would have once fallen into the fields of production development and overall marketing. But social media has made a profound difference, broadening the application and understanding of what content actually is. Social media has democratized things (remembering, of course, that there are positive and negative features about democracy, but that's a topic best reserved for another day). It's had a kind of "flattening" effect between the originator and the end-user, "flattening" the hierarchies and silos of departments.

You emphasize the importance of crystalizing a message and wrapping it up in only a few words? What is the main message of this book?

I would put it down into five words: **You Can Master the Art**. Content creation and promotion is an art, not a science. But it is also something not alien to any of us. *Explained!* tells you why, and, with those lessons, enables the reader to gain the confidence to become the pro that he or she already is.

Who should read this book?

The broader audiences are those interested in marketing, advertising, promotion, and many of the related traditional terms and practices. Any entrepreneur or small business person will find this book useful. And by small business person, remember that a dental practice or a law practice, for example, is also a small business. It all starts with an idea to produce something, to offer a service, to create something, to recruit people for voting or membership purposes. Whatever the case, it's all content creation and promotion.

ACKNOWLEDGMENTS

First, I must point out that the friendly and helpful staff at *Amazon KDP* were always available to assist with advice and tips, especially as regards some of the technical details related to publishing through that platform. This is much appreciated.

Amazon KDP is nothing short of transformative for the publishing world. Its existence, and the remarkable facility through which to offer an author's book virtually anywhere, opens opportunities that are truly inspiring.

The past and more recent experiences in my professional life have served as a foundation for the content of this book. Each of those experiences highlights the guidance and mentorship of some key individual. While the names and contexts are too numerous to itemize here, I am, nonetheless, constantly mindful of - and grateful for – each of their efforts to keep my compass pointed in the right direction.

Finally, this book would not exist without the tireless assistance and support from my wife, Josee. I suspect, at the very least, more than a few dinners might be in the offing.

PART 1
FOUNDATIONS

STEVEN CHRISTIANSON

Master the topic, the message, and the delivery

**Steve Jobs,
Founder of Apple**

STEVEN CHRISTIANSON

CHAPTER 1

LOOKING AROUND

Your breakfast cereal has a personality. Your insurance carrier speaks with an accent. Your airline has a family history.

And so they should. Personifying your product or service can give it a life of its own, separate from the business organization that designed and sells it.

The art of promoting something really boils down to creating that "thing" that people can identify with and relate to.

There is a reason why insurance agents plaster their personal photos all over their promotional materials (such as lawn signs, media ads or profile cards). It builds personality, which can build trust. The public persona of an actor is often quite different from who that person really is. The politician who runs for election, appears before the media commenting on such and such an issue, or plasters his or her promotional materials all over the place, but is usually not the same person as one would experience in private. Personal privacy is something we usually want to protect and share with only those who are close to us. The most compelling reason, though, rests in the ability to construct something more ideal, more sanitized and less fallible, something easier to control.

We all do it to a certain extent, whether we realize it consciously or not: when we build an online profile, with a personal image and a resume of our experiences, we "touch up" here and there, adjusting everything in the visual presentation, from lighting to skin complexion; we try to find the strongest possible words to communicate our job titles and responsibilities, making sure they cater to the audience, i.e. the potential employer.

Some people refer to this practice as the art of bullshit. But is it really so bad to put your best foot forward when presenting something, especially if we hope to make a lasting, positive impression?

Of course, there is a clear difference between someone who claims to have a university degree, when in fact that person really only attended a few classes. There is a difference between "beefing up" and utter fabrication.

The art of creating content and promoting it, be it a product we designed, a service we offer, or our very selves, is something we all do. This book is intended to help hone those skills we already have, thereby learning how to master the art of content creation and promotion.

But if someone is different in public than that person is in private, aren't we dealing with fabrication? Isn't the content we create a falsehood? A television commercial about an airline might depict a family member flying off to reunite with other family members. While the family is part of the fiction, that piece of fiction is presented as an example. The commercial needs to personify that example of what the airline does, otherwise it is unlikely that viewers will relate to the product. So there is an element of fiction, but one that is based on the very real products and services offered by the company, and one that virtually anyone who is able to buy an airline ticket can see himself or herself fitting right into the scenario depicted.

A key part of promotion is personification. An equally key part is the need for promotion to speak to larger concepts. Let's again consider the example of an airline company. We've probably seen at least one commercial of an airline company. What do they claim to be doing, as the commercial depicts family members reuniting with others? The company isn't just flying people from one place to another; the company is helping to bridge the distance of family members, to help connect loved ones, which then creates stronger bonds and familial relations within that family. It's a broader concept of not only what the airline does, but the impact it makes. And we've seen that impact many times: family members embracing the new arrival at the airport, with hugs and tears of happiness and joy. This is what the airline contributes to; this is the product and service it provides.

So we always want to remain mindful of the need to personify things as well as the strengths of broadening the concepts associated with what we do.

Of course, if everyone did exactly that, we would have limited product comparison. Imagine if every airline company touted its service as one that "brings families closer", there would be very little differentiation from one to the next. Which is why knowing what you do, who you are trying to recruit into your orbit of sight, and how you are different from others is always a critical first step – and an ongoing, periodic point of self-reflection. Airline ABC might bring families closer, while Airline XYZ might be geared more toward offering cut-rate fares, no-frills service and shorter flights. Two very different narratives of content; two very different forms of promotion.

Content creation and promotion are increasingly valuable tools in today's global, hybrid marketplace that features a combination of e-commerce and bricks-and-mortar, and can be essential skills for just about anyone trying to make a difference in his or her respective field of activity. As such, the flow of discussion in this book is more conversational, avoiding technical terms as much as possible. It relays experiences and lessons learned, and offers tips in a meaningful and relatable way.

The structure of discussion is organized in four parts: Foundations; Considerations; Perspectives; and Essentials.

The first part of our discussion begins with a focus on personality and why developing personality in your brand can be contributory to success.

Knowing and properly defining the problem or challenge in front of us constitutes the focus of the next section. While the theme recurs throughout the book, this section considers how action and self-reflection can work together to create a more fulsome understanding and definition of the challenge we face, and how an effective promoter must be an effective listener.

Branding as illusion constitutes the focus on the next section, where we delve into the tools that can help support your content.

Promoting social causes and issues, what many describe as advocacy, is more prevalent today than ever, and therefore rightly deserves attention.

Yet, corporate social positioning, although popular and increasingly evident, can be disastrous if not approached with extreme caution. That section and the next, changing names or monikers, both represent a trend seen among companies, towns, sports teams. Changing monikers and names, i.e. changing brands, is something a handful of high profile companies are doing, and the section on changing brands is both topical and illustrative of the exertive influence of social media advocacy.

It's difficult to talk about promotion, branding, sales, or any other dimension of marketing without at least referencing P.T. Barnum, so a special space is reserved for considering the lessons from a circus man, whom many regard as a prime exemplar in the art of promotion.

The next section is somewhat of a case study, highlighting the pros and cons of visual identifiers.

Two sections are dedicated to the use of music in promotion, one that provides a broad survey of music as a promotional tool, while the other section looks specifically at soundmarks and audio logos.

Digital integration and hybrid models are well developed in some markets, but not in others. Here we consider why that might be, and what it might suggest for a new product or service. We also consider the differences between social commerce and e-commerce, as well as their related applications in what is evolved as "the" new thing.

Authority, trust and influence are concepts discussed in several sections of this book, but receive dedicated attention as these concepts relate to power and the abuse thereof.

Self-reflection on the art of promotion, stepping back and asking, "who really cares?", steers the next part of the discussion. Here we address the perennial question: how do we know we're making a difference?

The final sections highlight key take-aways from this book, and reflect on their applications as well as their potential for innovation.

The overarching message in this book: there should always be a harmony between content and communication. Achieving that harmony begins with appreciating what promotion actually is, and demystifying the notion that you can't do it yourself.

Promotion is about more than just placing an ad, or putting up a sign in a window or in a parking lot. It is about understanding exactly you have that you want to promote, and appreciating the perceptions that people have about it. With those perceptions come stigma and sometimes misconceptions. Don't ignore these. Embrace these perceptions and stigma, understand them, and grow to love them. These are your barriers, your problems. Without knowing them intimately, you can never begin to know what it is that you are promoting, and just how you intend to speak to – and retain -- your target group.

You may want to "beef up" you online profile. You might be in the market for selling your services as an accountant, an electrician, or a virtual event organizer. Or perhaps you have become passionate about advocating for some issue or cause in your community or across the world. Whatever the case, the tools and tips in this book – at least one of them – will be useful in your endeavors, and hopefully become foundational to mastering your art of content creation and promotion.

Brand is just a perception, and perception will match reality over time.

Elon Musk,
Co-Founder/CEO,
SpaceX

STEVEN CHRISTIANSON

CHAPTER 2

IT'S AN ILLUSION

Someone recently asked me what I do (presumably, what I do to earn money that pays my living expenses on a daily basis). To which I replied, "I'm an illusionist".

In fact, we all are in varying degrees: parents to their children, job applicants to potential employers, a political candidate to voters, a real estate agent to prospective buyers, a teacher to students.

An illusion is a bend or warp in our perception of something. We assume one thing, but some aspect of a message has led us to focus on something else, whether visual, auditory or tactile.

When I was grad student, a few of us were ruminating over our upcoming sessions as junior lecturers and teaching assistants. It all sounded stimulating and prestigious. Yet none of us had any prior experience in standing up in front of a class of 80, 90 or 100 undergraduate students. Not only was the notion of standing in front of a crowd, and being the single source of the "show", more than just a little intimidating for us; we had no idea what we were up for. What if someone asked us a question and we didn't know the answer? Were we supposed to be experts in all matters of things related to the topic of the course? What were the expectations of that many students? So off we marched to the Dean's office. He welcomed the four of us into his less-than-spacious office, opened the window behind him, and proceeded to light a cigarette (those days are long gone). Listening to our worries, he leaned back, blew a puff of smoke out his window, and proceeded to explain to us that the answer was in the word "theatre".

Theatre and drama are at least 75% of everything we do. Those who understand and embrace this fact are those who become successful, he explained.

It was about the art of illusion.

This struck us as somewhat disconcerting. Had we been reduced (or promoted) to actors on a stage? Were we expected to "mislead" a bunch of students who were there to learn? In short, were we being asked to lie when a lie was the only available recourse? What was needed in this theatre of learning was a bend, or a warp, in how the students perceived us. In other words, as intimidated as we felt, we couldn't allow those feelings to be shared. Never let them sense fear? In a sense, that is very much the case: we were being thrown to the proverbial lions. We weren't expected to pretend to possess knowledge in areas where we clearly did not, or pretend to, have answers to questions. The idea was to shift the emphasis of perception by providing so much information, such a volume of reference material, and the image of profound expertise, and communicate the importance of absorbing the details for any future examination. A form of "awe", but without the accompanying "shock", to borrow a military reference.

Speaking of military, we find plenty of examples of illusion. In fact, perhaps one of the greatest acts of illusion is found via military style organization. The British bearskin hat, that black, furry tall hat that sits atop the red and black uniform of the Queen's guards in the United Kingdom (among other places), finds its origin in the battlefield. The idea was to make each soldier look taller, and thus more intimidating. This was bending or warping the perception of the enemy. The Maori of New Zealand use a different form of illusion: the Haka war dance. Synchronized men with tattooed faces move left, then right, yelling and chanting, with bulging eyes and distended tongues, conveying the idea that these soldiers are actually demon-like, are unafraid of anything, and are ready to consume your flesh. During certain battles of the American Revolutionary War and the War of 1812, it was reported that war cries from indigenous warriors actually repelled some invading soldiers. The content of the narrative, that spoke of flesh-eating wild men, coupled with the war cries (a kind of soundmark or audio logo, if you will – but more on that later), created a common perception of fear and terror. The illusion helped bend the perception from the reality, which was a contingent of men ready to battle, to a mental image of certain doom, thereby compelling the invading soldiers to retreat. Even the hair-raising feeling we experience on our necks when confronted with fear or danger is a built-in human illusion. Researchers today tell us that this feeling is a throwback to an earlier phase in our evolution when we were covered with hair. The raised hairs provided the illusion of increased size, that we appeared bigger than we actually were.

One aspect of corporate illusion has a different name: branding. It is part of an illusion, nonetheless.

The corporate entity needs colours, lines and shapes, and what emerges is a logo or a typeface. This then finds life in narratives and stories of all kinds, typically found in commercials or other media ads. Whether the goal is to make the company appear local and friendly, or global and all-powerful, what are essentially story-tellers and scriptwriters fashion an identity, giving it background and depth and context of character, giving it voice and thus an illusion of what the corporate entity or product actually is.

The more the illusion crystalizes into a focal point, an identity that people feel they can touch and relate to, the more sustainable the illusion is. In other words, the more powerful the brand identity and corporate image.

The examples are virtually endless: the *Jolly Green Giant; Allstate Insurance; Disney; Molson Canadian* beer; the characters Snap, Crackle and Pop; *Mr. Clean*; *Intel*; even George Washington. Each of these examples has a real entity and an accompanying image (virtual identity or illusion). Much has been written about each, so there is no need to delve into what each one is and how it transmits a personality. If you are interested, these are prime examples, and a simple *Google* search will generate ample information about how each of these identities were created, and how they helped forge and sustain their respective intended audiences.

Each is a focal point of a narrative and of a personality. And quite often, the narrative and personality usually have very little to do with the workspaces of the employees, the corporate by-laws or physical structure of the company that designed them or watches over their trademarks. Sometimes the narrative and personality we see, or that which we assume to be, has very little to do with who the actual person is or was.

Some illusion, or brand images, can take on a life of their own. The band, *KISS*, for example, is a personality and image quite distinct from the band's membership (which has evolved considerably over the decades).

I remember walking into the offices of *MAD Magazine* in New York sometime in the 1980s. I had the idea of a very busy workplace, featuring illustrators, writers, maybe photographers, a studio area, and the like. In fact, it was a very small office in a mid-town high rise that had the magazine's logo and visage on the wall behind a receptionist. In all, there were three or four small offices in there. It had the illusion of size, a personality with depth and context, yet was quite different when the proverbial Toto pulled the curtain aside to reveal the wizardry behind the illusion. Of course, the magazine signature character, *Alfred E. Newman*, is a content creation in itself. He never actually existed, despite having personified the magazine, despite having a history, and role in commentary, and a position of ostensible centrality and importance in the magazine.

You may feel that you're not an illusionist in any way. But consider if you've ever wondered which side of your face looks better in a photo, which shirt makes you look younger, or thinner, or healthier, or why a particular business suit makes you feel more confident when you walk into a team meeting. Ask yourself if you have ever tried to bend someone else's perception of yourself by trying to concentrate their focus on other details. You likely don't possess the information of a *Google* database – but your children probably believe you do. Which is why they tend to ask their parents every conceivable question on every conceivable topic. Now why would that be?

Don't raise your voice; improve your argument.

Desmond Tutu

STEVEN CHRISTIANSON

CHAPTER 3

SAVOUR THE PROBLEM TO ACH IEVE AUTHORITY AND INFLUENCE

Knowing a problem is harder than it seems. The main reason for this is that too many people are not effective listeners. It's only through attentive listening that we can correctly identify and define a problem, which can then help create a foundation for a potential solution. Don't fall in love with the solution; there are already too many solutions for every problem that exists. Instead, fall in love with the problem, savour the problem, learn to know it and understand it. With that knowledge, you will have the prerequisites of influence and authority. When you have the authority of voice and can measure a level of influence, you have what some might refer to as *power*, or at least a form of it.

This can seem a little heady, so let's step back a bit, and consider its application in politics.

Politics is that realm where passion can sometimes overwhelm logical strategy. It certainly occurs in many other realms as well, but the theatre of politics tends to consume significant segments of the daily news feeds. It tends to be something that many people can relate to, or are at least somewhat knowledgeable about.

Step back to the summer time-frame of 2020. Donald Trump was still President of the United States. Joe Biden was the Democrats' presidential candidate. But in the months leading up to that point, there had many aspirants wooing Democrat support. What was so appealing about Joe Biden at that time, and how did that man figure into the Democrats' strategy? Why was Biden a good choice to promote?

Passion aside, the Democrats looked at the problem, their problem. And what was that? The problem, as many had argued, was Donald Trump himself. Again, attempt to distance yourself from your personal views and passion. The problem was not actually Trump himself, but the issues that his supporters rallied towards, the motivators. The Democrats at that time in the electoral cycle seemed to have grasped a basic axiom: they embraced the problem, and crafted an electoral choice that spoke to *it* rather than finding a solution.

This can be somewhat confusing, admittedly.

There's a massive difference among political supporters, the politically engaged and active voter turnout. One person might have said that he supported Mr. Trump, but then doesn't turn out to vote. That's a supporter. You might find someone who is active and engaged, say, as a volunteer on the phones or canvassing at the doors. That someone could be anyone, a tentative or potential supporter who is curious and wants experience, or someone who doesn't have citizenship to vote but can take an active role in a campaign. Both the supporters and the engaged are critical to any election campaign. But election day is what the campaign is all about, and that's where the tally of voter turnout makes or breaks a campaign and a candidate. Who are the people who bothered to leave the house, stand in line, and cast a ballot? And why did they bother to do that?

Those two questions are fundamental, and should be asked during every electoral cycle (which is really a cycle of content creation and promotion). The Democrats seem to have asked those questions. What motivates a Trump supporter? What compels that person to physically get out of the chair, walk or drive to the polling station, stand in line – sometimes for hours – and cast a ballot (mail-in ballots helped alleviate some of that inconvenience, but that, of course, is a whole other story).

What motivates Trump supporters is the problem that needed to be savoured in order to begin understanding a path towards a possible solution.

And the answer, many would argue, is anger or frustration. Survey after survey confirms that those supporters were upset about a lot of things – hence the affinity with a slogan that promised to make America great again. But it takes something to really incite that voter to the extent that it would move that individual from the *supporter* category to the *active voter turnout* category. It appears that Hillary Clinton was a key factor in helping achieve that in 2016. A voter base reacted to Mr. Trump, supporting his approach, his words, and his ideas. That carried over to continuing to see a face, Mrs. Clinton's that personified their anger or frustration, thus providing ample motivation to turn out on election day.

Over the past few years, political analysts, myself included, from many countries, have made the cautionary note that the Democrats would commit political suicide if they chose a presidential candidate for the 2020 campaign who was flamboyant, charismatic, and magnetic. Why? Isn't that exactly what an action committee of a political party would be looking for in a candidate? One reason is that Trump supporters were already angry, and someone confronting their anger with panache and charisma could help to motivate them more, to turn out on election day and possibly give Mr. Trump a second term. A candidate with impeccable qualifications and experience, but who is more middle-of-the-road, non-offensive, like Joe Biden, wouldn't necessarily put a spark under the behinds of Trump supporters, wouldn't motivate them to vote *against*.

Of course, there is a double-edged sword in that sort of planning. The risk was that the non-offensive candidate might not even motivate Democratic supporters on election day, the only day that makes or breaks. So a masterfully-crafted choice of the first female and first non-white vice-presidential candidate was chosen to help propel significant Democrat supporters to make the effort and cast a vote. The risk, and there always is one, is that Harris might have incited the very anger that propelled Trump supporters in the first place. It was a well-executed option, and sufficient numbers of people "bought the product": non-offensive, older and middle-of-the-road balanced with youthfulness, charisma and inclusion. (In the final hours, there were other issues at stake, a topic which is acknowledged here, but deserves attention elsewhere.)

The Democrats clearly seem to have savoured their problem, fallen in love with the problem, and only then did they begin crafting a possible solution.

As was pointed at the outset of this section,

knowing a problem is harder than it seems. In deciding what content to create and how to promote it, one needs to first listen, reflect – and only then, consider how to define the problem. Even after you've done that, though, there will always be the need to periodically step back and reflect on your actions, and revise them if necessary.

Savour your problem, learn to know it and understand it. Once you have that knowledge, you are in a position to create content that has carefully reflected the problem, to reach out to your target group with authority, and influence their choices or their actions. The composite of that influence and authority, as we have seen through the example of the Democrats and Joe Biden, is *power*

PART 2
CONSIDERATIONS

STEVEN CHRISTIANSON

To convert somebody, go and take them by the hand and guide them.

St Thomas Aquinas

STEVEN CHRISTIANSON

CHAPTER 4

SOCIAL CAUSES AND ISSUES

How do you effectively promote a cause or issue? These things are always important (at least to one person), sometimes intangible, often emotive and compelling, and reside in a universe of other causes and issues that seems never-ending in size and quantity.

War, hunger, food security, poverty, climate change, affordable housing, inclusion, drunk driving, biodiversity, animal shelters, tax fairness, education, clean water. Your alma mater. Your church or place of worship. The local action committee or political party. A community service organization.

There are probably as many causes and issues out there as there are words in a standard dictionary: too many to count. More importantly, there are too many for anyone to really take. notice. So how do you raise the volume, get attention, recruit people to your point of view and maintain that momentum?

It's important to state up front what may be obvious to some readers. First, there is no single, cookie-cutter approach. Second, just because what you did worked well before doesn't mean it will again. The other important pieces we'll consider in this section are social media tools and advocacy apps, and whether or not these things offer any real value to your work.

Is promotion the same as getting attention? Consider: a person standing in the middle of a downtown street, wearing a clown costume and banging pots and pans, will certainly generate attention, and some of that attention will, no doubt, be recycled throughout the day on social or traditional media. The question is how to maintain that attention, and translate the awareness into action. What was the intention of getting that attention? Here is where things are not at as easy as they seem.

I was recently approached by a fellow who wanted to raise awareness of a disease he has lived with all his life, and one that would ultimately shave at least a few years from his expected lifespan. Who wouldn't be sympathetic? He explained that advances in medical treatments were happening in different parts of the world, and showing some signs of success. Those treatments, however, were not available in his country. Not surprisingly, he wanted to access those treatments, and he wanted everyone who also lived with the disease to benefit as well. He was passionate and committed to making sure as many people as possible learned about the disease he was living with, as well as the positive changes that these new treatments could make.

Yet he was a little unclear about why he wanted to do that. While he explained that treatments existed in other countries and should be brought to his, he wasn't altogether clear about his goal.

This is completely normal. Most people don't know what their goal is.

Did he want the public to support the need for medical treatment? If so, the problem was that the public probably didn't know much about the disease to begin with – hence the need for at least some education as a first step (which is a different type of content creation and promotion altogether).

But why bring the public into the equation in the first place, I asked. What if they say, "That disease is horrible. But there are so many other things that need funding"? End of story.

So let's assume for a moment that money had nothing to do with the outcome? Would the public then sympathize? Perhaps. Let's say they did. So what? How does that sympathy translate into the government updating regulations so that the treatment he heard about could be imported into the country? Should the messaging be targeted, then, to elected officials, who presumably could influence the process of writing or amending regulations? Or should the effort focus on the government bureaucrats who administer and manage the process? Things get even muckier. Just because there is access doesn't necessarily mean there is affordability. The treatment might be approved for import, but could he or anyone else realistically afford it? A level of subsidy would need to accompany the approval of the treatments to ensure affordability, and this, again, is an entirely different target of promotion.

Through that brief conversation, we identified several goals: public support; political support; policy change; access to the medical treatment; and improved lives.

So there were at least five goals, with many more objectives, and each of those goals entailing multiple steps. Yet he was hoping that a single solution existed.

Again, his approach in thinking is completely normal. Most people will say something like, "Well, I want to get as many *Facebook* likes for my petition." They'll explain their thinking, but few will acknowledge the need for these efforts to translate into action -- and a clearly defined action, at that.

Someone, somewhere, employed the petition as form of advocating their cause. That doesn't mean the petition is useful in and of itself. This brings us back to the need to recognize that there isn't a single solution, and just because it worked before shouldn't lead one to believe that it will necessarily work again.

It is also notable that as quickly as something can go viral through a social media platform or series of networks (which is discussed in greater detail in a later section), the demographics of those platforms can also change with amazing velocity. The platforms, networks and demographics should not be considered unchanging and secure. The primary user demographics for *Facebook* in its first few years were considerably different than those from, say, 2019. Those differences are even more augmented as a result of new and different groups of users being drawn to the platform as a result of some social or economic change – for example, a pandemic that keeps many people home.

So, what worked last year, on a platform that proved effective at that time, won't necessarily deliver the success you hope for when executed this year. The shifts in composition and demographics of users, and how those users interact, have been fascinating to watch, especially during 2019 and 2020.

The point here is to know the platform or the app. Look closely at the user demographics within the geography you hope to mobilize.

Which leads us to another important point.

How is it that anyone assumes you can mobilize even one person through a social media platform? Here's where we get into some relatively new tools and apps.

This book does not endorse one app over another. Also, you'll want to pay close attention to anti-spam laws and privacy rules in the area you're targeting. But here are a few interesting notes and examples.

Some apps that have shown effectiveness extend from the old-fashioned word-of-mouth form of promotion: Tell a friend, tell a family member. It's a personal, respected and trustworthy endorsement of the product, service, message or cause.

Team and *Outvote* are two recruiting and organizing apps that have shown levels of success in the United States. Then there are *UCanvass*, *Organizer*, and *Field Edge*, each with its comparative advantages. *Reach* is another that has some excellent features. There are many more. Most charge a monthly fee, which can be quite affordable depending on what you need.

Again, it matters whom you want to reach, and why that target group can help cause the change you hope to see.

As a closing thought in this section, I'm reminded of a lecture I once gave to a university class studying advocacy methods for various political and social causes.

I cautioned these young women and men to not rely exclusively on digital media simply because it's fast, newer or easy. Anyone can sign her or his name to an electronic petition as easily as pressing a button. There is really not much engagement or thought happening in the process. And the problem increasingly is that legislators know this, which is why e-petitions have limited effectiveness. Your Member of Congress or Member of Parliament knows that your electronic petition, despite its volume of digital signatures, has limited authority.

In contrast, two mail bags filled with letters or postcards, let's say, each hand-written and signed, represent considerably more effort, thought and authority. Like the closing court scene in *A Miracle on 34th Street*, when bags and bags of Post Office letters are presented to the judge, carefully choose the most suitable medium to parlay your message. Do it right, and you'll make a lasting impact.

STEVEN CHRISTIANSON

Speak to your audience in their language about what's in their heart.

Jonathan Lister, VP Global Sales Solutions, LinkedIn

CHAPTER 5

CORPORATE SOCIAL POSITIONING

Corporate social positioning is a relatively new thing. Companies typically set out to create something, sell something, or distribute something. It matters little whether the company is a sole proprietorship, a partnership or an incorporated entity. Regardless of the structure, or the product or the service, the company is established to make money. While generating sufficient revenue to cover expenses might constitute the making of money, if a company isn't making a profit, particularly over longer periods of time, the company's existence is limited. A profit is required at some point in the process.

Not so long ago, companies avoided unnecessary risk (at least in the sense that such risk could not be accurately measured). The voices representing the company, the president or the chief executive officer, namely some form of corporate leadership, typically sought to avoid ruffling too many feathers, upsetting too many people. Taking a political position, or social stance, was considered too risky and not consistent with the mission of making money. Why offend some when those people might someday be the very customers you need.

Gradually things have changed. In the 1990s and 2000s, companies wanted to be seen as ecologically responsible, sometimes having extended themselves to emphasize the environmental-friendliness of what they produced or sold. Being socially responsible, it turned out, was a good hook to sell more, and make more money. It became so widespread that even those not authentically "environmental" were adopting the stance. For those companies and productions, this was kind of an updated version of the old "new and improved" marketing gimmick (more on this later).

Then, many companies began to actually align their sponsorship with social causes. A typical Pride Parade in New York or Toronto is wallpapered with corporate sponsorship. Big banks and insurance companies, traditionally some of the most conservative of corporate entities, spend significant dollars to let people know that they, too, are inclusive and proud (and, to boot, are tapping into a significant market of wallets).

This is not to say that senior executives and corporate leadership isn't or hasn't been genuinely supportive of environmental or social causes. It's simply the case that the alignment of corporate messaging with a cause was considered excessively risky unless a significant demographic base could be delivered.

Things seem to have changed again.

The recent global demonstrations against racism, spurred in large part by the heinous killing of George Floyd in the United States in 2020, elevated issues associated with racism and colonialism to a global level never before experienced. In short order, corporate leaders and messaging started adopting a social stance. Notably, we heard remarks made by the Commissioner of the *NFL* saying that their previous position, that did not endorse the "kneel" by players during the American national anthem, would be adjusted to allow the "kneel" (this was something that many *NFL* players had exercised during the American national anthem, well before the George Floyd incident, as a way to heighten awareness of social and racial issues). Corporate social positioning was now officially responsive.

An equally fascinating example looks at the pressure for changing a name and the corporate response to that pressure: the threat by corporate partners to remove their sponsorship of the *Washington Redskins* of the *National Football League* if the team didn't change its name. Even retailers had threatened to pull team merchandise if the name *Redskins* remained. In due course, the name was eliminated, and the team played its 2020-21 season without that moniker. Corporate social positioning paved a path toward corporate re-branding and the changing of monikers. More on this topic in the next section.

Before continuing, I'll take the liberty of a brief commentary. *Redskins* is most definitely an ugly and pejorative term. It should never have been there, in this author's opinion. Interestingly, another team with an indigenous name also announced its plan to remove the moniker and re-brand. The *Cleveland Indians* will no longer be known as the *Indians*. In contrast to the Redskins affair, however, the term "Indian", can actually be referenced in legislation. (The logo and mocking imagery are different altogether.) Canada retains the use of the term, "Indian", in the very same context as that in the United States, with an *Indian Act*. The US federal and state governments use the word "Indian" in many legal references. In fact, the term "Indian", is used by more than just a few native communities and governments, themselves (or you may prefer aboriginal or indigenous). While this usage might not make the term any more appealing to some people, one should not confuse the fundamental difference. Or, is there a difference when it comes to "righting" past "wrongs"?

Along a similar line, we find another example in Canada, where a Canadian insurance company threatened to pull sponsorship of the *Edmonton Eskimos* team of the *Canadian Football League* if the team didn't change its name.

According to the company's July 7th, 2020, press release, the reason is as follows: "For several years, we have been a sponsor of the *Edmonton Eskimos* …. one of our core values is respect, which is founded on seeing diversity as a strength, being inclusive and collaborative. Guided by this value, in order for us to move forward and continue on with our partnership, we will need to see concrete action in the near future, including a commitment to a name change." (source: Belairdirect Insurance, Company Media Release, July 7, 2020)

The term, "Eskimo", is a pejorative term. The name should have been changed a long time ago. Interestingly, in February of that year, many months prior to the sponsorship media release cited above, the team issued a statement about consultation it had conducted with many stakeholders, including Inuit representatives, and informed via press release that there was no consensus on the need to change the team's name. Ultimately, the team announced that they will be moving forward without the term "Eskimo" in its moniker, and will be consulting the community to determine a replacement.

So are these examples of corporate social positioning that actually make an impact? In the Canadian example, the insurance company in question had been a sponsor of the *Eskimos* for several years, as their press release states. One asks why their corporate social positioning didn't call for a name change years ago? While one can argue that the outcome is the same and shouldn't matter, the issue, from a content and promotional point of view, can seem like a "me too-ism", rather than corporate leadership, and an alignment with social causes.

Here's where we get into the muck, as well as the risks of such alignment to corporate purposes. They can appear inauthentic, attempting to demonstrate but lacking in social leadership, and inconsistent with the personality of that corporation, that service or product.

While risky, this in itself is not insurmountable. So is it all that bad for the private sector and the business world to adopt social causes and social positioning, even if it rings of me-too-ism? After all, one could say that governments can only do so much, and that the private sector has a legitimate role to play, that it carries authority and influence, and therefore has a certain degree of power in communication. Perhaps.

This recent trend of companies and company leadership assuming social positions is also a recent topic of media discussion. On January 8, 2021, for example, *BloombergBusinessNews.CA* asked its readers the following online poll question: Do you support CEOs who speak out on situations? The question, in this instance, was asked in the context of the chaotic disturbances – and deaths – on Capital Hill in Washington, DC, that occurred days prior. More than 4,000 people took part in the poll. A whopping 68% said YES, that CEOs who speak out on social issues demonstrate social awareness. Fewer than a third of respondents said NO, that the focus of a CEO should be profit. While the poll was informal and certainly not scientific in any way, the results are consistent with the rising trend in corporate social positioning, and the view that private companies should use their authority and influence to promote social causes.

Let's be careful with this, and remain mindful that the ultimate purpose of any company is to make money -- and that their very existence must be based on the realization of profit. There are instances during which a social momentum helps provide a fresh perspective on a company's goals, mission, and sometimes even its identity (or branding). This is not only inspirational, but can represent significant opportunity for the company or organization.

As we have seen with some social causes, the importance of the issue can be fundamental to some, but find only a finicky and temporary appeal among others. Moreover, corporate leadership, unlike political leadership, is both unelected and unaccountable to the public. So any authority and influence they exert on social causes must be received with a healthy mix of optimism and caution.

Your brand is what people say about you when you're not in the room.

**Jeff Bezos,
Founder & CEO,
*Amazon***

STEVEN CHRISTIANSON

CHAPTER 6

WHAT'S IN A NAME

What's in a name? Sometimes much more than a brand. In the previous section, we considered the use of corporate monikers and their impact on people, and how corporate social positioning may or may not play a part in that impact. This section continues on this path, and employs the license of satire to help illustrate the opportunities and the risks related to a moniker or brand.

Some names, nicknames or other such monikers can be ugly, insulting and hateful – even if those who use them do so without malice. Using them, even in nice ways, doesn't make it any better. Polite racism is racism nonetheless.

We discussed how the *Washington Redskins* of

the *NFL* dropped the name, *Redskins*. A new one will be announced at some later date. Red skin: Now that one should have been obvious; and, in fact, it was for many people. Better late than never, one might say. The *Edmonton Eskimos* and *Cleveland Indians* are also looking for new monikers. For many people these are monikers that are best left in the past. What we have yet to discuss is how far the rationale of changing names can or should extend. There is also the issue of cost. While the cost of not changing the moniker may be high, and the benefits reaped by doing so (through merchandising opportunities) could be substantial, there are some very real out-of-pocket expenses associated with a re-brand. Team uniforms, stadium signage, online properties, and traditional assets like stationary or presentation materials, represent just a few areas affected.

Today's trend in re-branding, like corporate social positioning, can be inspirational. But let's exercise a bit of caution when approaching this topic. Let's step back, reflect and ensure that we have properly identified the problem. Where is the line between what should and what should not be considered acceptable for a brand or a moniker? How evenly will people apply a consistent rationale of evaluation as to whether or not a name or image is offensive enough to warrant change?

Some names and images are clear cut. Others are less so.

Make no mistake on the matter: if we are to venture down the path of rewriting names of things or places, we had better have a clear conscience and accepted understanding as to what is and what is not included.

Now we're going to apply some levity to the discussion. Let's continue with the names of sports names.

Aside from Edmonton, is anything other than the name or image from the *Canadian Football League* potentially hateful or disturbing to a culture or a people?

The *British Columbia Lions*, as a name or an image, could hardly be deemed offensive by anyone. What about the choice and significance of the colours? Orange was chosen for its association with the Orange Order, members of which were original founders of the team. The Orange Order sees itself as defending Protestant civil and religious liberties; however, critics have often accused the Order of being sectarian, triumphalist, and supremacist (this author takes no stand on the matter). Could this potential source of controversy offend anyone?

The Winnipeg Blue *Bombers* have an interesting history. The name, Bomber, is actually associated with a boxer (brute force), while the imagery used by the team evokes a fighter pilot. A bomber is a killing machine, something used in war to effect death or terror. Is this potentially offensive to anyone?

Similarly, the *Montreal Alouettes*, although

possibly referencing a bird, have made clear that the name honours a World War II air squadron. These units were designed and built for war. War rarely occurs without bloodshed and death. Should this name be allowed?

So that's a third of the entire *Canadian Football League* that possibly should consider new names, new brands.

Let's move on to the *NFL*. Aside from the obvious *Redskins*, is there anything else? *Buccaneers* and *Raiders* as teams seem quite acceptable, yet these historic terms have associations with violence, pillaging and theft. The *Bills* are named in inspiration of Buffalo Bill Cody, who, according to legend, was noted for his effectiveness in killing native Americans (or Indians, as the term was used in his day) and upwards of 4,200 buffalo, an animal that became precariously close to being put on the endangered list.

Can we find anything in the *National Hockey League*?

Well, it's a good thing that the *Hartford Whalers* no longer exist. This name could be said to have glorified the hunt and slaughter of the greatest mammals of the sea. The moniker in Ottawa is associated with one of the biggest empires of the world, the Roman Empire, which is historically featured by slavery, massacres, mutilation, torture and death by public spectacle. The *Ottawa Senators*, while not evoking much more in its name than a stately chamber of elders, uses the imagery of ancient Rome. Should this be brought into question?

The *Columbus Blue Jackets* reference the Civil War in the United States, one of the bloodiest on record. The *Chicago Blackhawks* may claim to be honouring first nations, but do they have explicit consent by any native representatives? The *Winnipeg Jets* clearly pay homage to military air forces; and again, these things are built to protect, but also to fight and cause death. Some Canadians view the word, Canuck, as a slight or an insult, so the *Vancouver Canucks* may want to rethink things. Then we have the *Las Vegas Golden Knights*, a reference to the owner's military college days.

The fun continues with major league baseball. In addition to the *Indians*, the *Atlanta Braves*, like the *Blackhawks*, claim to be honouring something or someone. So again, did they consult those people and get approval for its use?

The *Tampa Bay Rays*, previously known with the word "devil" in the name, rebranded since their early days of play. Some people, it turned out, were in fact pretty darn upset about associating their team with something demonic or evil.

Then let's look at the *Washington Nationals*. Certainly nothing about the logo or the name could disgust anyone. What about those mascots? Characters designed to evoke reference to the War of Independence, something both gruesome and, for those of us north of the border, an historical bookmark to the very first refugees taken into Canada.

The *Texas Rangers* also have some colour in their past: the Porvenir Massacre is a particularly brutal part of the history of the real contingent of Rangers, and not one that is overly glorified by Mexican Americans.

The fun doesn't stop with sports teams. Dildo, Newfoundland (yes, it is a real place) or Swastika, Ontario (it's also real) could also fall under this review. The historical meanings are different than what people associate the names with today. But certainly one could be offended by either of these place names. In fact, people have been offended. Does that offence warrant a re-brand?

The worrying element here is how far this rationale extends. A momentum towards sanitizing or cleansing, as one might call it, has serious potential for reaction as opposed to thoughtful consideration. Such reaction could very well take the form of censorship, be it historical or sociological. What's worse is the increasing tendency, especially throughout social media, to not only judge and condemn anything from the past, but to attempt to erase it. This "Cancel Culture" has been growing in the past few years; this culture that positions itself as cancelling anything considered disagreeable, that collectively shames the holder of a brand or a moniker. Regardless of whether or not one agrees with the momentum of the "Cancel culture", this online "movement" has made an undeniable impact, and represents a trend to watch.

Even the first name of this author, Steven, could be offensive to some. Its origin is ancient Greek, which directly translates into wreath or garland, and references St. Stephen, the first Christian martyr, who was stoned to death, while also carrying an association to the specific wreath of thorns on head of Christ during the time of his crucifixion. An honour and a part of faith for some, a significant part of historical narrative for others, and yet for even some others -- a reference to one of history's most notorious episodes of physical torture and torment. For me, it was simply the first name of the *Six Million Dollar Man*, and he was just plain cool. And on the topic of the *Six Million Dollar Man*: herein we have an entire brand built around concepts that were temporal and, therefore, subject to antiquation. To relaunch and remake the production would require a reconceptualization of the protagonist and his relative market value. But I digress.

A recent online columnist argued that a company, be it a sports team, a food processor or a financial services firm, should actively look at changing its name or imagery if even one person whose culture or history has association with it, feels hurt or offended. If that's the case, and I don't think it should be, that's a whole lot of rethinking, rebranding and redesigning.

Which, on the upside, I suppose, offers great opportunity for the world of content creation and promotion.

PART 3
PERSPECTIVES

If we are not customer-driven, our cars won't be either.

Ford Motor Company

CHAPTER 7

THE IMPORTANCE OF PEOPLE: LESSONS FROM A CIRCUS MAN

There so many issues at stake today in launching a new product or service. The majority of start-up businesses fail within the first year. Moreover, traditional bricks-and- mortar businesses (those things that typically composed the main streets in our neighbourhoods and towns) are, at best, living a precarious existence. So with all these challenges, with so much going against the efforts to advance your product, cause or service, are there any basic principles in which we can still place our confidence?

This section is a little different, in that its main purpose is to share some reflections in the context of the memoirs of P.T. Barnum.

Sometimes old wisdom seems so sensible that one would think it were as common as air. Yet it is such common sense that we sorely miss in today's world.

P.T. Barnum, generally known as the circus man, and remembered for more than few hoaxes, was a masterful promoter and creator of narrative. Regardless of one's opinions or views about circuses, the name, *Barnum and Bailey Circus*, is widely known, and its origins date back to 1871. That is one heck of a legacy for a company. As for the man, himself, he excelled at nearly everything he engaged in professionally.

One reason contributing to his success is that he knew he was in a business that needed people, customers. To need customers, you must know how to reach out to them, speak to them, capture and maintain their attention. Barnum was a master of his craft because he knew people, and, more importantly, he enjoyed getting to know and understand people. Whether we call it a love of people or a dedication to service, the importance of that dotted line between the business and the customer must never diminish. Barnum wrote in his memoirs: *Be polite and kind to your customers. Politeness and civility are the best capital ever invested in business. The truth is, the more kind and liberal a man is, the more generous will be the patronage bestowed upon him.*

Picture yourself venturing into a store, in person or online, whether to browse or to make a specific purchase you already have in mind. When the chat window pops up, welcoming you and any questions you might have, you get that human connection as well as the feeling that you are considered both welcome and important. You might experience a similar feeling when you walk into a physical store, a small shop, let's say, and the clerk behind the counter looks up, smiles, and welcomes you, sometimes thanking you for the taking the time to visit and shop.

Yet how many times in your experience, does the sales representative, who is sometimes the owner, ironically, not even bother to look up or say hello?

These are observations on common courtesy; a foundational principle in how to promote and sell. It's funny, though, how manners and common courtesy seem less evident today when businesses are flogging their wares. And economic analysts wonder why some businesses go under?

Courtesy cannot guarantee success; but it is the key ingredient in guaranteeing that you know and fully understand the paramount importance of people.

Barnum knew people because he liked getting to know people. He was also an elected official in Connecticut, a position difficult to secure without knowing how to connect with people. He had a keen sense of what it took to get a message across to people, how to make the desired impact.

He intuitively knew that you couldn't recruit people to your cause or sell people a product or service until you had their understanding. In fact, he often said that *the* object in promotion is to make the public understand what you've got to sell.

Remember our friend, whom we discussed in an earlier section that talked about social causes, that fellow who was used as an example of how most people tend to omit steps in their thinking? The public needed to understand his medical issue, how it impacted his life, why treatments could help and how. They needed the narrative, the content.

So how does one, according to Barnum, work towards making people understand what you're promoting?

1. He cautioned that the reader of a newspaper does not see the first insertion of an ordinary advertisement. That does not constitute a failure, but a simple fact. So, there must be a "second insertion".
2. The second insertion he sees, but does not read.
3. The third insertion he reads.
4. The fourth insertion he looks at the price.
5. The fifth insertion he speaks of it to his

wife.
6. The sixth insertion he makes the purchase.

The "insertion" of today could be in the form of a traditional print advertisement in a newspaper or magazine, as it was in Barnum's day. It could be in the form of direct mail, be it a flyer, postcard or unsolicited letter. Today, it could also mean a radio ad, a television commercial, paid message on a news/content channel, an audio spot in a podcast or audio book, any form of content (still image, audio, animated or text) in any one of the online platforms out there (be it a more common-styled website or multi-platform social media feed).

Remember, it took six insertions for a promotion to transform a potential target audience member into an active buyer in Barnum's day. So one shouldn't be surprised that in today's world, featured by masses of multiple forms of messaging in multiple directions simultaneously, one or two paid appearances of your message on *Facebook*, *Twitter* or *Reddit* just isn't going to cut it.

Establishing a presence takes time and perseverance. Making a connection with customer requires courtesy and an authentic interest in people.

We need to accept that we won't always make the right decisions, that we'll screw up royally sometimes – understanding that failure is not the opposite of success, it's part of success.

Ariana Huffington,
Founder & CEO,
Thrive Global

CHAPTER 8

PROS AND CONS OF VISUAL IDENTIFIERS

One of the most unpredictable, one of the trickiest, efforts in promoting your content, is found in knowing which "song" is the "hit". By song, we refer to anything that becomes the hallmark, the signature, the one "thing" that speaks to an audience. It's fascinating how often that "thing" happened unintentionally, somewhat accidently. That "thing" is the visual identifier. The band, *Rush*, never consciously embarked on using the "starman" image as its "thing". It happened. It became the visual identifier. The United States Senator, Bernie Sanders, probably never sought out to brand himself with hand-knitted mittens. It just kind of worked. Those simple woolen hand-warmers inadvertently became his visual identifier.

A visual identifier is that something that exemplifies your personality, your brand, your image, what you stand for and represent. While it can be a logo, a visual identifier quite often is something else entirely. We'll get into a discussion in this section about what visual identifiers are and how they can be important by looking at a specific case with the Government of Ontario and its recently designed license plates.

As with jurisdictions around the globe, Ontario requires drivers to affix an alpha-numeric identification plate to all moving vehicles. Plates have been issued by the government since the advent of the automobile.

Over the decades, the design of the plate has evolved, featuring different colour contrasts during different times. The main image, though, has always been a crown, an image that recalls the heritage of the Province. At times, the crown has been left-justified, while at other times placed bottom-centre. Until recently, that is.

In 2019 the Ontario Government announced that the Province's vehicle plates would be redesigned with new technologies, and the government would begin issuing these to the public in February of 2020. Newer technologies on plate design were being introduced in various jurisdictions. Since there were also quality concerns with the previous batch of the government-issued license plate (under a different governing party and premier), it was deemed an appropriate time to update the design as well as to adopt the new technology.

Preliminary images were released in early 2019. Aside from partisan-tinged commentary, there really weren't any significant public issues with the design of the new plates. The province's colour combination of blue and white was prominent, the updated slogan gave a nod to nostalgia, and in addition to the crown the design featured an updated logo of the Ontario government, a stylized trillium.

So Ontarians were being introduced to an updated brand, an updated logo. No one at that time, however, could have guessed that the plate itself would become a visual identifier of the government as well as its missteps or successes.

The updated plates were released according to schedule. Brand new plates with brand new designs and brand new quality began replacing plates with old designs and quality issues that had been issued by and associated with a previous governing party. The new plates were becoming a kind of hallmark of a brand new government and what it was all about. That's the good news. The unfortunate part of the story is just how powerful the plates as visual identifiers had become.

The new plates could not be read in the dark, according to officials in local police departments, as well as national border officials. The new product was faulty.

The government's first reaction was denial, then blame-shift, then acknowledgement that complaints were being reviewed, to finally a disclosure that the plates were, in fact, defective, and would be recalled and replaced.

As gnawing as this would have been for officials in the Ontario government, as upsetting as it might be for anyone issuing a new product accompanied by a re-brand, mistakes happen. But in this instance, the mistake had the power to become a visual identifier.

What is the purpose of a vehicle plate, a licence plate on your car or truck?

The plate is part of system of identifying the ownership and registration of a vehicle. It certifies legally that the vehicle is road-worthy and otherwise not questionable, and this information is linked to registries in insurance companies, police and government databases, and border systems.

Without this system, we would have uncertainty and chaos surrounding car ownership, accidents, liability, sale and purchase of vehicles, to name a few issues. So it is evidentiary. It is proof. It is a tool that contains sets of data and information.

What else is a vehicle plate? It's a little piece of advertising, sometimes displaying your name, company or favourite cause, which, by the way, can also serve as a source of revenue for the government.

Is it anything else? It says to people, especially when we're driving outside our jurisdictions, "hey, look where I'm from". So imagery associated with your home, a famous landmark, say, will be used to "shout-out" about your country, province, territory or state. Perhaps one of the most effective shout-outs in plate design and imagery comes from Canada's Northwest Territories. Heck, the entire plate is cut into the shape of a polar bear.

So getting back to the purpose of the plates: did the purpose require updating? The answer is yes. They needed to incorporate improved technologies; to remain consistent with North American standards; and to replace outdated technologies and defective products from previous runs.

Replacing defective products, which the previous run of plates certainly represented, should have resulted in a better and improved product. The public administrators and political bosses have experience on this matter. They've been overseeing the manufacture, design and issuance of vehicle plates for many decades.

Yet the result was not an improved product. The result was failure. What's worse, that failure is evident on multiple levels. One can reference the evaluations and feedback from police, who claimed that they could not read the plates at night, as well as those responsible for radar and photo systems, and from border security. A total recall and replacement announcement confirm the level of failure.

The failure can also be seen from a branding and promotional perspective, because the power of the visual identifier was so strong.

The efforts on the policy front and the efforts on the communication front were not in harmony.

As paradoxical as it might seem, visual identifiers can help propel a narrative or company or government, but those very identifiers can serve as constant reminders of failure. Had the mistake been immediately acknowledged, perhaps a different outcome could have emerged.

Herein is the most serious risk in not knowing the power of an exemplar of your company as a visual identifier. The failure in updating the plates was reinforced because the product itself – something attached to the front and rear of moving vehicles -- is visual, easily identifiable, one that has action, personality and image all sewn together into one crystalizing moniker. Moreover, the vehicle plate is, as a brand, a moving advertisement. Wherever that vehicle travels, whenever someone sees that image, the misstep or success is reinforced.

When planning a re-brand or a new narrative, you also have to factor in possible failure and what the ramifications and costs might be. When the risks of success or failure can be branded, and serve as a visual identifier, the questions associated with "What if we tried to ...?"

become as important as the appeal of the imagery or the quality of the narrative. Plan your actions as harmoniously as you can.

As for the role music can play – a song choice can reinforce the particular message the brand is trying to convey and demonstrate a brands' personality.

Alex White,
Co-Founder & CEO,
Next Big Sound, Inc.

STEVEN CHRISTIANSON

CHAPTER 9

MUSIC AS A PROMOTIONAL TOOL

Brands and logos are usually thought of by many people as visual functions of content creation and promotion. This is not surprisingly, since these things typically do manifest in something visual. Did you know that audible tools can promote a product, service of cause, and sometimes with greater effect? Think of the commercial jingle, an audible promotional tool you've likely heard countless numbers of times. But music has far greater potential and a deeper history in promotion than through the use of commercial jingles and melodies.

Among all the things that music can represent to a listener, music is also an important tool in promotion. Music has been used to woo crowds for centuries. From parades, church hymns, and circuses, to street organ grinders and commercial jingles, music captures attention, it helps cultivate appeal, community and affinity, and it ultimately contributes to selling, recruiting or retaining, as the case may be.

Music has been used in product promotion for about as long as anyone's memory serves. Much has been written about this, so there's little need to explore that application of music as a promotional tool in this book. However, there are many other promotional applications of music.

The use of music as a promotional tool in politics and related political messaging is particularly interesting.

Without question, Americans have mastered this medium, and still serve as a benchmark. An American election is as much a pageant as it is an exercise in democracy. It's so effective that people want to be part of it. The US President even has an unofficial anthem, Hail to the *Chief*.

A considerable quantity of messaging has found its voice in music: *Yankee Doodle Dandee, Give Peace a Chance, Sunday Bloody Sunday, A Change is Gonna Come, Ohio*. The songs themselves often transcend their intended meanings, and have become embedded as popular pieces of music. Yet, these are just as political as the anthems played at a White House celebration.

The use of live musical performance has also been commandeered to raise awareness and help change policy. This process is known as advocacy, which we discussed earlier, a form of content creation and promotion centered on causes and issues.

Farm Aid in the United States was started by Willie Nelson, Neil Young and John Mellencamp in 1985 to raise awareness about the loss of family farms, and to raise funds to help keep families in locally-based, family-owned and -operated agriculture. Concert festivals were used to lure the crowds, transmit the message, and generate donations.

In Toronto, in the early 2000s, when the city was listed on the steer-clear-of list by the World Health Organization due to a respiratory virus, the SARS outbreak, the use of live music, and its accompanying crowds of fans with money to spend, was corralled to help create a different narrative about health safety in the city. And it turned out that performances by the Rolling Stones, AC/DC and Rush (plus another 20 or so performers) was an effective salve against the economic downturn associated with SARS. Nearly half a million people attended, helping generate massive media coverage the world over. Music was used to help change the narrative, to create new content, and to promote that messaging.

Another interesting use of music in a political format was recently found right inside the United Nations headquarters in New York City. This was seen through lobbying efforts, another art of content creation, persuasion and promotion.

As a brief aside, lobbying, simply put, refers to the promotion of a message, aimed directly at government or elected officials, with the intent of introducing or changing a policy, program or law. The term, lobbying, by the way, originates in the British parliamentary tradition, and was used to describe the practice of conducting conversations with members of parliament, particularly cabinet ministers, which at one time took place in the "lobby" of the entrance to the House of Commons.

While lobbying takes a different form in the UN, it is lobbying, nonetheless. Every now and then, elections are held for membership on one of the dozens of committees in the UN architecture. Delegates representing countries and non-governmental organizations (NGOs) appeal to other delegates attempting to persuade their votes. Frequently these appeals to colleagues include incentives ranging from special events that offer cultural cuisines, to educational materials, posters, trinkets and souvenirs, and – yes, music. These appeals usually have some effect. Who wouldn't want to take in a live musical performance with some hors d'oeuvres and cocktails and the end of a long day of deliberations in a UN meeting hall?

In a recent bid for new membership of the Security Council, several countries were vying for the coveted and prestigious seat. Tastes and samples of various products from each contending country were offered to those considering the candidates. Most relevant to this discussion, tickets to musical performances by artists of each country's delegates were distributed to voting members.

The Irish wooed their colleagues with U2 tickets, while the Canadians tapped into the power of Celine Dion. It was thought by many in that round of voting that Canada would surely secure a seat (not solely because of the tickets, or course). Alas, it turns out that tickets to a Celine Dion performance wasn't enough of a draw for voting delegates. Ireland, on the other hand, pushed its candidacy for the Security Council seat with overtures that involved free tickets to Riverdance and a U2 performance. Ireland ultimately won over the votes.

Did the choice of musicians affect the outcome of voting delegates' decisions in any real way? Not likely. One would venture to guess that delegates would have been captivated by a performance by either of these musical powerhouses, and that more substantive policy issues would have steered the voting outcome.

One thing is certain: your selection of music that is intended to get your point across must also appeal to those making the ultimate decision.

Music can be a powerful tool to catch attention and win over a potential customer or vote. It has the power to embody the message you want to promote. Music can be one of your most effective transmitters. Music has also the potential of outlasting your campaign, regardless of whether that campaign was tailored for an election, a new product launch, or securing enough votes to win a seat on the UN Security Council.

The traditional "jingle" was typically a short, original composition designed to highlight key words and, most importantly, grab a potential customer's ears in a catchy way. This is the type of promotional tool that many people are most accustomed to hearing. Other musical pieces will borrow and rearrange an already composed and published piece, usually one that was popular at the time, and use the rearranged version for the promotion. This method is a little riskier, in that the marketing teams responsible for the campaign typically try to tap into the "cool" factor of the song or the artist; however, they had better have some first-and, experiential knowledge about that artist or song. Of course, a negative outcome of a piece of music is that it utterly turns off an entire segment of the population.

While the benefits can be monumental, the risks always exist for any piece of music. Music is emotive, and those emotions and context associations of music can easily go either way.

Repetition and perseverance also play a factor when considering the choice or form of music. It's one thing to recruit a band to play a one-off performance to raise awareness of a cause, but altogether quite a different matter for an ad campaign in high rotation play that uses a rendition of a previously popular song.

Like anything that is potentially powerful, approach the use of music as a promotional tool with understanding and healthy caution. Know why you want to use music in your messaging. What do you hope to achieve with it? Is it the most suitable promotional tool for your content, message and campaign?

STEVEN CHRISTIANSON

There's one powerful branding tool that has been generally overlooked — or perhaps undervalued — by most marketers: sound.

Harvard Business Review

CHAPTER 10

SOUNDMARKS AND AUDIO LOGOS

In the previous section we discussed music applications in the art of content creation and promotion. This section will consider the use of something related, but quite distinct and even shorter in composition than a commercial jingle or anthem: the soundmark and the audio logo.

An audio logo is a tool that is actually a sound trademark. Sound is used to perform the trademark function of uniquely identifying the commercial original of products or services. They are known by several names: audio logo, sound trademark, soundmark, and probably a few more. So what exactly are these things?

You're probably more intimately familiar with

these tools that you might think.

Imagine yourself in a movie theatre sometime in the 1980s or 1990s (if you're old enough). The coming attractions were done. Commercial ads had played. The film was about to being – but first, views experienced something else: a soundmark.

The *THX* soundmark was first introduced in the early 1980s. The sound was used on trailers and played in *THX*-certified movie theatres. It was used to let the audiences in movie theatres know that the film they were about to see used *THX* technology, that the theatre was equipped to give the audience a full *THX*-quality sound experience. There was no catchy music, no words in the piece. The total audio running time was less than 20 seconds. It was a sound wave that built to a crescendo, then faded out. It was produced and owned by *Lucasfilm*.

Over time, viewers anticipated that part of the experience. The soundmark became associated with the beginning of a film. The sound itself was cool to listen to and experience as it swelled to that cinema-filling rush, engaging the full realm of the audio system. It inadvertently also let latecomers know that the film was beginning.

That soundmark is one of the audio trademarks with a longer running time. Whether they were ran for two seconds or twenty seconds, they did much same as a visual logo -- performing the function of uniquely identifying the product or service.

There are many more examples, and some go back decades.

Take the *20th Century* soundmark. Even if we might not correctly identify which studio owns it, we instantly recognize the drum arrangement as identifying a movie studio. For generations of film buffs, the *20th Century* audio logo has introduced the company's product and reinforced its brand through an assortment of complementary media.

The sound logo is one of the tools of sound branding, along with the commercial jingle, brand music, and brand theme. We hear them as a distinct sequence of sound.

One of the earlier examples of this type of branding was used by *NBC* in the United States. The *NBC* "three chimes" served as a form of network identification. Television viewers knew that once those chimes sounded, something promising, something entertaining, and presumably trustworthy (since its broadcast license had been granted by government), was about to begin play in their living rooms.

More recently, *Home Box Office*, or *HBO*, has used its soundmark prior to the beginning of every episode of each show it has produced and broadcast or streamed.

The *Netflix* audio trademark falls into a similar category. Again, we hear that sound at the beginning of every Netflix show we watch. Not only is it the acoustic equivalent of a visual logo, it complements the animation of the logo, thereby doubly reinforcing the recognition of the brand, and taking content creation and promotion to even more refined levels.

Soundmarks have also blossomed in the realm of consumer goods.

Intel computer chips uses a very simple, four-note soundmark with a total running time of less than a couple of seconds. This classic soundmark by *Intel* signalled to consumers that the computer they were considering was built with *Intel* chips. You only needed to hear the sound, and you knew what it was. Its simplicity makes it a very powerful example of audio branding.

Another example of audio branding in consumer products is seen in the mobile phone. Telephone advances in the 1990s and 2000s developed at an incredibly fast pace. Differentiation is critical to success for any company and product. One of the early leaders, *Nokia*, chose to distinguish itself through its soundmark ringtone. This ringtone is one of the longer compositions in audio branding, but has become classic and, in some ways, has taken on a life of its own. Not only has the short melody been used as a promotional tool in television commercials, but it was the default ring-tone for the phones themselves, reinforcing the brand on the screen, on the radio, and through the telephone handset, lending itself to a very different user experience.

As we discussed in the previous section, melodies and jingles have been used to promote products and services for generations. Many would argue that one of the enduring reasons that the US presidency and US elections have traditionally been so appealing to people is the use of melodies and themes. As discussed, these, too, are forms of branding and brand reinforcement; but the soundmark, or the audio logo, is a bit of a different *tune*. They allow us to *hear* the logo without even *seeing* it. They tend to be shorter, more concise.

Unlike a jingle or melody, intellectual property protection for soundmarks and audio logos is still comparatively new, with much discussion and debate continuing around questions such as, "Can Company B put a trademark on a simple sound, or a single note or two?" It was only in 2012 that the *MGM* lion's roar was given support by the US Federal Court. Interestingly, in that same year, the Canadian Trademarks Office allowed for the registration of soundmarks. Even today, while soundmarks are registrable, and soundmarks can receive protection in law, the process is still less than cut-and-dried than is the case for more traditional trademarks and copyrights.

During the advent of the commercial Internet, the world wide web, in the 1990s, some early versions of websites featured soundmarks in an opening page. And as promotion becomes more digital, audio branding becomes more important. You'll want something to distinguish and identify your podcast, your website or blog, your *YouTube* channel. It can become a key part of the personality, and a very powerful identifier with the potential for multiple uses.

As with many things in life, simple can often be better. Yet, while it might sound odd, creating a four-note sound logo can sometimes be even more challenging that a four-line, 30-second musical jingle.

So next time you're listening to the radio, or watching a commercial, movie or TV show, see if you know the brand just by hearing the soundmark. Try to become aware of these tools when visiting websites or listening to podcasts. Think about what that sound tells you about the company's content, and what it is trying to promote.

PART 4
ESSENTIALS

STEVEN CHRISTIANSON

If I had to guess, social commerce is next to blow up.

Mark Zukerberg, CEO, *Facebook*

CHAPTER 11

SOCIAL COMMERCE

Online shopping has exploded in volume and popularity, especially at an accelerated pace since early 2019; and so, too, have the opportunities associated with innovation. New products and promotional tools can certainly be innovative. A more exciting breed of innovation, though, is when we see a convergence of worlds, an integration of the digital realms, a form of social commerce or e-integration.

Put simply, social commerce happens when someone sells something directly on social media. The entire experience, from locating what the customer wants, to comparison shopping, purchase, check-out and letting others know about your choice, all takes place on one platform. This is the integration that makes social commerce really innovate.

E-commerce, on the other hand, has been around much longer. This occurs when, say, a store puts its catalogue of products on a website or app. The customer visits that specific location, selects, purchases, and checks-out. The customer closes the app or leaves the website.

Social commerce places the customer at the centre of everything, and there is no need for the customer or user to leave. In contrast, e-commerce offers a technology or service online, allows the customer to visit, but, most importantly, like a bricks-and-mortar store, provides no further incentive or reason to remain in that location once the transaction is complete. Social commerce is a more fulsome, more robust, form of e-integration.

YouTube, *TikTok*, *Snapchat* and *Instagram* lead the pack in social commerce. You probably guessed that Millennials and Generation Z constitute the majority of users. Video is the primary form of content, and short, snappy clips, at that. Then, through the video content, social media users are connected directly to a brand by simply touching the screen. The best feature of social commerce? The fact that everything is built around mobility: it operates across multiple platforms in an integrated way, and is tailored to the mobile device. E-commerce means offering a product or service online, quite often through what started as a website and later became transposed onto a dedicated app. E-commerce lacks the social media experience, whereas social commerce blends e-commerce with social media experiences.

An enthusiast of digital innovation would rightly be fascinated with this growing trend. In Western markets, social commerce is trending towards big bucks. Yet, that same enthusiast would be doubly fascinated to see the trends as they have developed in China. While we're moving closer to e-integration in the West, the convergence of the realms that give rise to social commerce are really still in their infancy, and have not yet transcended generational boundaries in a substantive way.

China features a fascinating integration of live streaming, content creation, promotion, retail, person-to-person communication, and banking. In this integrated mix, the consumer is central, where all else radiates from that consumer-centric position.

In contrast, western economies, while featuring astounding forms of innovation, still have "silos" that haven't yet broken down. Finance is a silo separate from content streaming, and both are separate (though at times can be coordinated) from retail. In the West, innovation is driven by technology, which is a very top-down approach.

The result of the continued existence of silos implies distinct efforts of content creation and promotion.

The market is more highly concentrated in China than in many other places. As well, one finds a significantly higher percentage of mobile users in China (98% of internet users connect through mobile!). While the computer, the processing chip the world wide web ushered in massive changes in the West, it was the introduction of the integrated mobile device – the gadget that combines the features of a telephone, a device for shopping, ordering, paying, sending condensed messages, taking photos and watching movies – that began making the most profound changes. Ask any official at the United States Postal Service or Canada Post why their revenues had plunged so severely during the 2010s. The mobile device really did change everything, and its mobility and technology opened a new landscape.

China did not evolve as the West did from a base of consumerism. In the West, while there was a sort of convergence of technologies, there were primarily physical in nature (for example, the use of cars and their relationship to getting customers to shopping malls). This is all bricks-and-mortar. As a testament to this fact, today, according to data from various consulting houses, more than 300 million people in the United States have 30 times as many malls as China does – with 1.4 billion people.

There's still plenty of physical shopping in China, but the high proliferation of mobile technology, as well as greater economies of scale and intense urbanization that create cheaper delivery options, add another level of attractiveness for Chinese consumers.

The Chinese consumer culture started at a different time and from a different place. That culture has grown in tandem with the proliferation of technology. Social networks and shopping blended together to a far greater and more effective degree than anywhere else. The Chinese consumer culture has evolved with technology, with the consumer positioned as a central figure. Everything else radiates from that point.

The outcome treats content creation and promotion as an integrated process. The vendor relies on the social network of family and friends, who can vouch for the quality and efficacy of the product. Social influencers are integrated as key pitch people, of a sort. The buyer of the product is encouraged to stream reviews and demonstrations, even short dramatic skits. As long as a mobile device is at the ready, and in China those devices reach 98% of the population, the integration works equally well for the remote farmer as it does for an urban jewelry maker. Content creation and promotion are integrated through every part of the system.

This direction in social commerce engages consumers in ways previously unexplored in the West. Some of this is due to Western regulation, which maintains the separation of silos (there is certainly no shortage of anti-trust actions); and some is the result of higher relative prices in the West. Western consumers have a different economic culture. Creating content about the product you purchased, and promoting that content through multiple ways and formats, comes as second nature to many consumers in China. In contrast, far fewer consumers in Western countries hold as much confidence in sharing purchase patterns and spending habits with those who inhabit the digital world. For now, this behaviour is concentrated among the youngest generations (although, the very groups with tremendous buying power).

The harmony of digital and e-integration in China helped create its foundational ascendancy of social commerce. There is some evidence that shows similar trends, though to limited degrees, in a number of African countries as well as those of the Middle East. In these markets (many of which have been categorized as "emerging" or "developing"), research is showing that the "trust factor" is more important. Social commerce may well become a dominant model in these markets as well, but those forces that instill and reinforce confidence and trust appear to be particularly important. We get into a deeper discussion of trust and authority in later sections of this book.

Will we see social commerce develop to a degree as robust as in China? For that to happen, change would be required in many fronts: regulation; consumer behaviour; the number of firms, etc. We have seen convergence of industries and sectors in Western economies: banking and securities brokerage; finance and real estate; retail and credit; and some consumer products with communications (the voice-activated home assistant, for example). But the silos that exist in the West are still considerable. Alternatively, could China see a dampening of the appeal and popularity of social commerce? Is this "thing" still so new that its novelty might diminish with the aging of their society?

Rapid advances in technology can at times be accompanied by surprisingly rapid changes in social or consumer behaviour (the shorter-term effects of the coronavirus global pandemic on work, school and shopping suggest that some social and consumer behaviour can adapt remarkably fast).

The younger generations in the West may help usher in changes previously unseen that could eventuate towards, or resemble, e-integration and social commerce. These are the consumers who have grown up with, and are situated at the centre of, technology. It is they who seem to have a more intuitive, more integrated approach to shopping, banking, voting, streaming – and content creation and promotion.

Above all, you want to create something you're proud of.

Sir Richard Branson, Founder, Virgin Group

CHAPTER 12

TRUST AND AUTHORITY

Previously we discussed how the "trust factor" plays a bigger role in the development of social commerce in some markets compared to others. For example, while the influencer is central to the effectiveness of social commerce, a user's trust in the authority of that influencer can determine how and to what degree a market of social commerce will develop. Which brings us to the question: why do people believe what is told to them? Why do they trust the content of the message and the source of the promotion?

Let's revisit the earlier section where we considered the lessons of P.T. Barnum. Although far from fact, popular legend has it that Barnum immortalized the phrase, "There's a sucker born every minute". If that's the case, why would anyone trust his advice, much less dedicate a few pages of a book to discussing it? Herein is a great example of thrust and authority. How does anyone know for certain that Barnum ever spoke those words? Whose authority that tells us that he disparaged the customer to such a crass extent gives this legend so much credibility? Interestingly, one should note that while popularly attributed to Barnum, there is no actual evidence that he spoke those words. On the contrary, Barnum was an individual who elevated, not disparaged, the status of his customer. Yet someone at some time has led most people to believe that Barnum was the man who spoke and immortalized the phrase. Why did people believe it to be true? On whose authority?

We have an innate quality of recognizing, perhaps even *wanting* to recognize, the authority of others: "It must be true if was printed in the newspaper."; "They reported it on the evening news."; "It was published on a website." Even the social media platform, *Reddit*, seems to acknowledge the implicit trust people have in the authority of others: "Where did you hear that," asks one person to another. "I *Reddit* somewhere." Clever.

Doesn't the old cautionary note, imploring that the buyer beware, teach us anything? Let's again visit Barnum's steps in the promotion of content. The reader, or listener, or customer, really has nothing at stake until the point of purchase, or the decision to consider a purchase. Prior to that point, the message or narrative is one of informal authority. When the purchase is made, we leap to recognizing the source as formal.

While this distinction is important, there is still the tendency among most people, it seems, to want to recognize the authority in others, be informal or formal. The only difference with the recognition of formal is that the reader, listener or customer becomes active in the process, specifically that a transaction, in some form, occurs. The transaction has a value, and it takes formal authority for someone to hold that level of trust.

When someone has the authority of voice and can measure a level of influence (for example, by the transaction), we then have what some would refer to as power.

The notions of trust, authority and influence in the efforts of content creation and promotion have virtually unlimited potential. So compelling is the potential that the schemer and fraudster have attempted to secure his or her position in the market. Knowing that people want to recognize authority, we have a field wide open for tricksters, profiteers, scammers and the like. They have taken many forms and have occupied virtually every field and profession, twisting the art of content creation and promotion, abusing trust and authority, to their advantage.

In 1962, a "technical expert" informed television viewers in Sweden, who were watching their country's only TV channel, how to "convert" the image on their TV screens into colour. He explained that a simple nylon stocking could be stretched across the black-and-white screen, which would bend light in a way to create the effect of colour. Viewers might then need to "adjust" the effect, by simply moving their heads to the left or to the right. Thousands of viewers, it was later reported, were frantically searching their homes for extra pairs of nylon stockings to stretch over their TV sets. While the entire episode was later attributed to an April Fool's joke, the content and the way it was promoted tapped into people's innate quality of recognizing the authority of others. "It was on the evening news, and an expert explained the process." Ergo, it must true.

Years prior, the radio broadcast of *War of the Worlds*, narrated by Orson Welles, went live across the United States. The radio program was aired as fiction, a radio drama, and listeners who heard the program in its entirety were aware of that fact. However, for the thousands who tuned in mid-program, the content sounded more like a news report. The producers never intended to trick anyone. Alas, more than a few reports of suicide were made that evening and the following day, as some listeners could not bear the thought of aliens from another world landing in towns and attacking their civilizations. The authority of the broadcast, and the measured influence it had, culminated in a form of power that few could ever have predicted.

There are many more examples of friendly pranks and unintended hoaxes, some with unintended consequences. Then there are the intended abuses that many of us have experienced or know about: everything from spam emails to boiler room telemarketers. Many of these operations target specific demographic groups, such as older seniors, people with language barriers, and low-income households. Yet other target groups can be none of the above. The film, *Boiler Room*, provides an expose of shady brokers and traders of various financial investments. Their targets are professionals who have a bit of surplus cash. These targets, medical doctors and dentists, are convinced – over the phone, by a voice they had never met in person

– to put their money in investments that turn out to be bogus. The film is a great example of how trust and authority can be abused in the creation and promotion of content. *Matchstick Men* is another in which telemarketers convince people that they had won a "grand prize". All that was needed to claim the prize was the transfer of funds to the telemarketers. The amount, call recipients were told, was roughly equal to the taxes that would be due on such winnings. In this film, people's bank accounts are emptied, prizes were, of course, non-existent or a flaccid version of what was explained to the "prize winner", and the operation regularly closed shop and resumed under a new name, in a new location. It sounded real, people wanted to believe and trust, and the confidence men who ran the scheme abused the power of how to bend perception, how to promote the content to accentuate what the target wanted to hear, and how to "get out of Dodge" with their pockets full.

One of the more recent types of fraud that play on the authority of content and promotion are the tax collection calls that many Americans and Canadians receive. The caller will tell the "target", that person who answers the phone, that significant income taxes are owed. The caller would then cite multiple, obscure and always false names, regulations and laws from that country's tax authority. Imagine receiving a call from your tax authority: it's likely going to make you feel uncomfortable, worried perhaps. In this scam, callers are told that if they pay even a fraction of the alleged amount owing, through a direct transfer or the opening of access to their bank accounts, that all matters against them would dropped. Ultimately, thousands of people, and many thousands of dollars, have been the subject of this kind of fraud – the kind that abuses people's innate quality of recognizing the authority of someone or the medium in which the message is transmitted.

Regulatory oversight and the imposition of punitive measures help address some of these concerns. Furthermore, the advent of "fake news" has prompted more than a few decision makers at social media companies to dedicate resources to identifying and removing such content from their platforms.

However, as long as there is opportunity to do something that generates an economic gain, a corresponding percentage of people will identify that opportunity as a potential to scam, scheme and abuse.

At this point the attentive reader might be thinking back to the section on illusion, on the bending of perception. Isn't that act of bending perception really just an abuse of authority and people's trust? To an extent, it is; to an extent, we all do it.

The key take-away here highlights both the opportunity of making an impact with our content and promotional efforts, as well as the responsibility we have to ensure accuracy and integrity, and to identify and avoid any unintended outcomes.

If your product is "new and improved", let people know how exactly it differs from the previous version. If you are offering free access to your online services, don't hide the clause that informs customers of monthly charges that will later appear should explicit cancellation not occur (negative billing). In short, don't get carried away with accentuating something and, in the process, creating and telling a *non-truth*. Your most important resource – your potential customer, reader, listener, audience member – is the keystone of your efforts, be it to personify your blog, recruit people to a social or political cause, or attempt to reinforce your corporate identify and presence in the broader social realm.

While technology is a prime mover in developing the innovation and opportunities of markets, trust is the eternal enabler.

Advertising isn't a science. It's persuasion. And persuasion is an art.

Leo Burnett, Founder, Leo Burnett Company

CHAPTER 13

PUTTING PERSUASION INTO ACTION

A potential customer must be informed about your product or service. This involves a variety of communications and techniques. Whatever your mix, your efforts ultimately help inform a customer whether or not to buy, as well as which supplier is best at that time.

A producer of the best product available won't be generating very much business if no one knows the product exists. In other words, don't run off and build "it", believing that by its very existence your customers will flow. It is often said that the balanced mix of your efforts should be 20% on content creation and 80% on promotion. But promotion must be more than the passing of information. It must be persuasive and it must differentiate. It matters little whether you are launching a new jewelry business online, constructing an election campaign for a political candidate, or advocating for a change in an existing law or regulation, you must be persuasive and you must differentiate.

In previous sections we discussed various components of helping differentiate your product, service or cause. The fact is, when persuasively promoting, you need the right mix of techniques. We also highlighted the importance of tailoring your mix to your product and target audience at a particular time. In other words, to reiterate, don't replicate past mixes simply because they worked well before – ensure that they do again! Also, you must be in the "long game", that is to say, to understand and appreciate that your efforts – as Barnum said a century ago – are cumulative, so much so that such efforts may even seem routine. Persistence and perseverance are never old-fashioned.

When starting your considerations of persuasion, sometimes it is more useful to first consider the negatives. What are the disadvantages of the methods of promotion that you are considering? Is there a reason you feel that a particular tactic is more suitable to the target group you're looking at? Can one tactic be measured with greater accuracy than another? What are the important differences for you when considering between a low-budget or no-budget tactic compared to a full suite of techniques. Can you not afford to provide a free sample, trial or membership?

As the title of this section implies, persuasion is only one part of the picture; closing the sale is equally important, as this outcome is the all-important measure of success.

Many people claim to be uncomfortable with the notion of "sales". The fact is, like the art of illusion, we are all engaged in sales, whether we know it or not. The art of persuasion is only as useful as the end result: action, agreement, buy-in or a sale. We sell ideas, proposals, our resumes, even our online dating profiles. We try to persuade; we aim to seal the deal or get the buy-in. The buyer is simply the manifestation, the persona, of the outcome we hope to achieve. The buyer can be a potential customer, the potential employer, the voter, your child or spouse, the potential date.

The effectiveness of your persuasion directly results in the degree to which your desired outcome is achieved.

When considering the tools of persuasion, the use of in-person tactics should never diminish in importance. Buying a new home represents a huge item of consequence in people's lives. Nothing can replace the in-person connection that a real estate agent brings to the experience. In fact, that's a big reason why realtors include their faces on their promotional materials (also reinforcing brand, and solidifying confidence and trust). Another arena where the importance of in-person contact is paramount is in election campaigns and voter engagement. A town-hall meeting or door-to-door canvass establishes and reinforces the personal connection that speaks to issues of trustworthiness and confidence. No amount on online or virtual interaction can replace this key piece.

That said, let's consider the digital world and how various online properties can advance or hinder your cause.

Never underestimate your existing contact list. That list is much bigger than most people assume. An old rule-of-thumb once used for assessing the potential effectiveness of insurance associates was to see if the candidate for the job could list 100 contacts – because each of those contacts is a lead. One hundred contacts? Who has that? Well, most of us have at least that. All names likely are not consolidated in one list. The volume increases as soon as you consider the networks you may not even think about: people who attended school, college or university with you; people from a sports team, drama club, musical band or hobby group; people in your neighbourhood; people at your present job as well as past places of work; people in your professional associations or church groups; your medical doctor, your dentist, your lawyer; your local elected officials; your mail carrier; your family members and their family members. This list goes on. And very quickly you will realize that your list is much, much bigger than you once thought. The list expands again for those people who are active on social media, when considering every contact, friend and follower. Starting a base with your own contact list is hugely important.

For many online efforts it is useful to start backwards by first looking at what you hope to achieve. First consider who you want to reach (and don't say "everyone"). Do you want media coverage? Asking end-of-game questions like these helps tailor your content to the medium and the types of people who frequent those platforms or networks.

A legal service provider will have a different audience than someone promoting environmental issues, and a retailer of pick-up trucks will likely be dealing with different issues than the owner of a bicycle shop. A candidate for elected office will want to differentiate between those online groups who chat, debate and criticize from those who are active and are actually eligible and inclined to vote. Someone seeking to raise membership in their church or club would be wasting a monumental amount of time by focusing primarily on existing membership. Your content will vary depending on the path you take.

Make it go viral, some will say. Ok, so what does that mean? Many people tend to embrace the lingo without really knowing what the words mean or how to achieve the result. Virility, online, simply refers to the re-propagation of content. It certainly helps things if that content is sensational in quality or features images that must be "shared". Make no mistake: getting something to go "viral" isn't about having content in the can, so to speak, then making it so. It doesn't happen on its own, despite how important you feel your content may be.

Persuasion can happen anywhere. Online, today, there are a handful of forum-styled network applications that stand above the rest: *Twitter*, *Facebook*, *YouTube*, *Reddit*, *Pinterest*, *LinkedIn*, *TikTok* and *Instagram*. *Anchor*, catering to audio content, will be discussed separately. Note that all times cited below are EST, and are the result of usage and applications with dozens of projects and clients.

Additional information about each of these services, such as date of launch and focus of activity, is found in the section, "Take-Aways, Questions and Answers", near the end of the book.

CONTENT CREATION AND PROMOTION

Twitter is an excellent place to find reporters looking for breaking news. While many people post opinions and thoughts, *Twitter* is an effective vehicle to share useful information and articles about a topic, targeting a specific reporter you know covers and writes about such content. This also generates a certain amount of attention on you and what you're doing. In an earlier section we considered the individual who wanted to promote awareness of his disease. In this instance, that individual could send an article to a health reporter or a public affairs columnist, and talk about how people who also live with his disease are affected differently through the pandemic. This type of content promotion is different, eye-catching and useful, and can generate additional content, helping elevate coverage of his cause.

> *Twitter*: Lunchtime on Wednesday.

When is the best time to post on *Twitter*?

From 12 noon to 1 pm. There are many apps and tools that help organize your posts, and these are best scheduled just prior to that 12 noon to 1 pm timeframe, the traditional break for lunch. Weekdays tend to receive a higher volume of activity, with Wednesdays in particular generating significant engagement.

Facebook can be highly useful for sharing any content that is featured by an image. It is particularly good for helping introduce users to something, which, in this forum, typically requires that extra, targeted push – paid placement. While it can result in action, its main benefit is helping people know you are there. *Facebook* is also effective for building networks within the network by joining or creating groups. There is also a growing social commerce component to *Facebook*. Keep in mind that the demographic on *Facebook* is somewhat older than it used to be in its early days; correspondingly, the younger demographics of Generation Z and the Millennials tend to converge more heavily in other platforms. Content-heavy material won't find a robust audience on *Facebook*. The word "face" in the name is used for a reason.

> *Facebook*: Mid-afternoon on Sunday.

When is the best time to post on *Facebook*?

Typically, especially for business pages, schedule your posts between 1 pm and 4 pm, while trying to avoid Tuesdays. Mid-afternoon on Sundays generate the highest level of engagement.

YouTube

YouTube is primarily known as a visual medium (although it has a rich and growing volume of audio-only content). As such, depending on your product or service, it can be useful for reviews, demonstrations, how-to's, lessons, conference content, and short docu-content. Ad placement on *YouTube*, as with many other online properties and apps, is also an excellent tool for spreading and reinforcing awareness. But it's the original content you upload, or that which is created by influencers to talk about your product, cause or service, that can help give momentum to the views and shares.

> *YouTube*: Just before the weekend.

When is the best time to post on *YouTube*?

Shortly before people will tend to watch anything. Viewers generally browse video content during the evenings, so make sure your content is up and ready. The best time to post is between 12 noon and 4 pm, typically on Thursdays and Fridays. Heavy traffic occurs on weekends.

Reddit has the advantage of user pages, groups and sub-groups. Ad placement can be targeted in very specific ways. Custom content can be easily posted and shared. If you engage and activate your existing networks, *Reddit* can really open up potential: like a hub of mini clubs, each with their own little websites (so to speak), you'll find just about everything there, but take the time to become familiar with membership rules, as well those for posting, ranking by Karma, and user engagement. *Reddit* certainly has immense potential, but many have attested to its unique quirks and nuances.

CONTENT CREATION AND PROMOTION

> *Reddit*: 7 am Saturday to Monday.

When is the best time to post on *Reddit*?

Early mornings. Saturdays, Sundays and Mondays, between 6am and 9am, is when most Redditors are most engaged.

Pinterest

Pinterest embraces the idiom, "a picture is worth a thousand words". You don't have to be stuck with finding pretty or provocative images. A pie chart, graph or other info-graphic can serve the purpose here. Pins and shares are common on *Pinterest*. The realm of *Pinterest* originally was predominantly female. Today, the gender gap of users has closed considerably. Although it still is the go-to place for cooking-related content, a simple topic search will yield a broad spectrum of interests.

> *Pinterest*: 9 pm on Saturday.

When is the best time to post on *Pinterest*?

Posting during the evenings tends to work best, between 8 pm and 11 pm, with Saturdays standing out. Avoid standard work hours during which to schedule a post. Although the gender gap has closed considerably, mothers tend to represent a highly active demographic.

LinkedIn used to be described as the professional's version of *Facebook*. If the aim of promotion is you, this network can be very effective. Getting a job, or recruiting a candidate, has become one of the strengths of *LinkedIn*. This is also a forum with company- and professionally- oriented content. People are not typically sharing family or vacation photos on *LinkedIn*. However, let's say you wanted to promote a new home office innovation, this network may be right for you. Again, as with most networks, offer something useful, something of value to the users. Don't just blurt out "here's my product or service … now buy it."

CONTENT CREATION AND PROMOTION

> *LinkedIn*: Mid-week, mid-morning.

When is the best time to post on *LinkedIn*?

Mid-morning during the middle of the week. Tuesdays, Wednesdays and Thursdays show the best results, typically from 10 am to 11 am.

TikTok

TikTok is fun, but the capacity to spread a short clip among several thousand people in a couple of minutes is very real. This network caters to custom content that is easily sharable. Eighty-five percent of businesses already use video as a marketing tool. The primary user demographic on *TikTok* is notably younger, so video content that is humorous or features animals constitutes the lion's share of content. This platform is young in another way: it was launched only in 2018. Influencers tend to reside here in larger numbers (as well as *YouTube*), so one form of promotion attractive to many at this point is paid promotion by an influencer. Pay attention to your user demographics on this platform. For example, you might be able to spread the message about your political candidate rather effectively, but the users in the network might be too young to vote.

> *TikTok*: Tuesday at 9 am or Thursday at noon.

When is the best time to post on *TikTok*?

The answer to this one really does vary. It kind of depends on who you are, what type of content you're promoting, and where you want to promote it. That said, there are metrics that show when user engagement is high: Tuesdays at 9 am; Thursdays at 12 noon; and Fridays at 5 am. While the times shown here are EST, keep in mind that users are global, so a little time-zone arithmetic is required sometimes. Also, pay close attention to analytics in the app, which will provide account holders with a decent overview of usage, engagement and other demographic-related information.

Instagram (now owned by and a part of *Facebook*) has really evolved into a useful platform for small businesses, restaurants and cafes, and group feeds for sports teams, music groups and tv shows. This is image-based, using video, GIF and still imagery. Want to promote your newest menu item or the film showing on a certain streaming network? *Instagram* is ideal for this type of content promotion, incorporating the ability to feature a GIF of the film or a photo of the meal. Easy for sharing and complete with hashtags, *Instagram* is perfect for that one-a-day dose of content from your team.

> *Instagram*: Saturday at 5pm.

When is the best time to post on *Instagram*?

Saturday at 5 pm is a great time to schedule a post. That said, you'll find effectiveness by posting on Monday, Wednesday and Thursday either between 11 am and 1 pm or 7 pm and 9 pm. Most recent data show that the highest volume of user engagement is Wednesday.

Anchor by Spotify

Anchor is a podcast creation and distribution platform. Your podcast episodes can be as frequent as your wish. Although length really isn't an issue, a good pod is not more than 10 minutes (and even half of that is better). Every company, every person, has something to say. *Anchor* lets you record and upload. *Anchor* then publishes to a wide range of streaming apps. Some companies use this content to augment (even replace) the corporate blog. One local elected official in this author's city has a weekly program that features interviews with owners of local businesses, student athletes, seniors ... you name it. As a delegate of the people, listeners hear him respond to various opinions, providing a virtual town-hall. The podcasts are easily shared and tagged. For that local politician, the podcast helps reinforce his brand and profile in the community, positioning himself as a listener, one who asks questions, one highlights the importance of people, and one who embraces new ideas and innovation – all essential qualities when considering the electability (or saleability) of the candidate.

> *Anchor*: Wednesday or Thursday at 2 am.

When is the best time to publish on *Anchor*?

Schedule your publishing times for 2 am either Wednesday or Thursday. Although significant distribution is immediate, it is best to allow some time for a fuller distribution to take effect. Thursdays, throughout the pm, show higher levels of listens and downloads. Like many of these platforms, *Anchor* provides analytics and very good information about listening patterns.

Remember, everything used in combination with each other, engaging users (or the audience) regularly, as elegantly as possible, is your ideal target. Also remember, much of this work in social media and digital content and promotion is still trial-and-error, to a degree, and it can evolve and change quite rapidly. Anyone out there who professes to be an expert in social media really is an enthusiast with some heightened, experiential and applied acumen. As mentioned at the outset of this book, the content herein is also sharing experiences, and considering lessons learned from attenuated application and enthusiasm.

If you remember that you already have a significant base of potential outreach contacts and leads, social media can help provide the trajectory to amplify your message, expand your reach, and promote your content. First know what you have (in other words, what is that content), why you want to promote it, and which specific group you want to target. You're already well-versed in sales. Just import those skills of persuasion into your project or campaign.

Don't be afraid to change the model.

**Reed Hastings,
Co-Founder & CEO,
Netflix**

CHAPTER 14

HOW DO WE KNOW WE'RE GOING IN THE RIGHT DIRECTION?

Ongoing self-reflection is critical in content creation and promotion. We have to pause occasionally, and ask ourselves, "how do we know we're moving the right direction, especially when so many things around us are moving?". The world today is moving faster than it ever has.

The Shifting Economy. We've been observing, and to an extent experiencing, a shift for quite some time. The ubiquity of mobile devices and the explosion of e-commerce are not only hallmarks of the shift, but they helped usher in newer convergences. It is these convergences that represent the biggest shift in our economic surroundings. The steady decline of traditional bricks-and-mortar retail over the past several years is a symptom. It often takes a "disruptor" to enter the picture and really "blow things up"; that disruptor has been the global coronavirus pandemic (which began to make its impact felt in late 2019). Stay-at-home orders, shutdowns and lockdowns opened the aperture of a wide social acceptance of relying heavily in mobile devices and e-commerce, to such an extent that the shift manifests in widespread closures of entire chains of previously thriving retail empires. While one might point to the shutdowns as the biggest reason for the decline of traditional, physical retail, the trend was evident prior to the pandemic, and the trend of widespread closures of physical retail will not likely reverse in the foreseeable future.

The growth of social commerce. Convergence is the key word of our times. The more we see the convergence of social media and e-commerce, the greater will be the opportunity for social commerce. We're seeing this convergence to a degree. Yet, as discussed in earlier sections, a market like China's is fundamentally better suited for this type of trend. That said, few could have predicted the degree of disruption caused by the global pandemic. That disruptor could yet help motivate a further breaking down of the silos that characterize Western markets, thereby helping to usher in greater convergences of the elements that create social commerce.

The Ascendancy of Digital Currency. Crypto currency, like *Bitcoin*, challenges the paradigms of traditional money and banking because of its ability to circumvent such systems. Crypto currency relies on technology instead of the authority of the state that banks rely on. According to *Wikipedia*: *A cryptocurrency is a digital asset designed to work as a medium of exchange wherein individual coin ownership records are stored in a ledger existing in a form of a computerized database using strong cryptography to secure transactions… \typically a blockchain that serves as a public financial transaction database.* We are also seeing the early signs of digital versions of paper money currency, traditionally controlled and issued by central banks. The disrupting factor, the pandemic, has served to accelerate the consideration of issuing an official digital currency in many countries. Regardless of when digital and crypto currencies become the norm, we are at a point today where hard-copy money (paper money) has likely reached its summit.

The impact of social media. Earlier we discussed the impact of social media on a company's brand. The influence is undeniable. We also see social media's impact on our traditional sources of news. Giving rise to "fake news", social media has slowly become the predominant source of news and current affairs information for many people. Anyone today can be a reporter, broadcaster or current affairs columnist (each of which contribute significant to the formation of public opinion). While traditional news organizations typically had fact-checkers and proof-readers, today's growing spectrum of social media news rarely has any of these "checks and balances". Another impact is found in revenue loss: traditional news organizations have lost significant revenue to social media sources of news and information – to such an extent that many traditional providers of news in several countries have worked in coalition to changes their country's rules more in their own favour. The authority and influence of social media on news and current affairs content creation and promotion are both measurable and profound. For example, the impact of *Reddit* users on the stock market and stock valuations in February 2021 illustrates the authority and influence of social media; moreover, this example highlights the features and characteristics (sometimes antiquated) of the current system. These changes will continue.

The Internet of Things. Convergence is accelerating even on the home front, in our personal lives. AI-driven voice-activated assistants are common devices in people's homes today. These provide not just answers to questions we might have about the price of gas at the nearest service station or the price of roundtrip airfare; they can provide the news of your choice, weather updates and personal calendar reminders. They can control a wide range of functions, from your audio and video libraries, to shopping, home appliances and security systems, even placing voice calls or composing and sending text messages. And these systems are not limited to the home. AI systems, many of which are voice-activated, are now basic features in just about every automobile. Regular service appointments for your car are as much about updating the operating systems as they are about servicing the physical components of the vehicle.

The volume of change around us can be as exciting as it is dizzying. So how do we know we're moving in the right direction, making our desired impact, with the creation of our content and promotional efforts? Are we really making any difference?

Despite the changes we're experiencing, and will continue to do so for several years to come, the principles that underpin our work never diminish – principles such as establishing a presence, differentiating what you have to offer, relating to your intended group through personality and narrative, and remembering the importance of persistence and perseverance.

One of the greatest benefits of the increasing proliferation of digital systems is data. We're able to measure and monitor metrics and analytics as never before. What's more, much of this data is instantaneous and self-driven at any given time of the day or night.

With that readily available probity of numbers, there might come a time when you see an impact or a measure that you didn't expect. Your cause might have recruited more seniors than ever expected, for example. Your product video might be viewed more frequently in a part of the world that you never considered. This is opportunity. So grab it. Shift the focus and respond accordingly.

What about negative feedback? PT Barnum (again) once said that there is no such thing as bad publicity. The point here focuses on "making what you can with what you have at your disposal".

Several years ago, prior to social media and related apps, a local, relatively pricey restaurant received a scathing review by a well-known food and restaurant critic, and one that was published as a full page column in a national newspaper. The owner was devastated. He had only been open a couple of months, invested much of his life savings, and worked daily on the floor, greeting customers and overseeing operations. He didn't know what to do. Instead of shying away from what he considered bad publicity, he was advised to embrace it. How? Reprint the review from the newspaper, enlarge it to the size of a poster, and hang it in the front window of the store where passers-by could read it. He couldn't change the fact that the review had been published. So, he embraced its perceived negative publicity, and used it to help change the narrative. Passers-by became curious about this relatively new restaurant that was promoting itself with such a scathing review. His business revenue increased.

Recalling an earlier section in this book, remember to properly identify the problem by embracing it and savoring it.

Amid all the dizzying changes and shifts that have been happening around us, also try to remember the notion of creative destruction. According to *Wikipedia*, the term "creative destruction" was coined by Joseph Schumpeter, an Austrian economist, in the 1950s. Also known as Schumpeter's Gale, *Wikipedia* informs that the *"gale of creative destruction" describes the "process of industrial mutation that continuously revolutionizes the economic structure from within, incessantly destroying the old one, incessantly creating a new one"*. As a theory of economic innovation and the business cycle, creative destruction occurs when a new innovation or technology essentially renders obsolete a previous technology, system or innovation. Innovation and creativity in the economy create something new, which displaces something outdated. There are countless examples, but one that many people can likely appreciate is found in the obsolescence of video rentals. An entire service sector, that featured networks of video rental stores, based on the technology of the video cassette and DVD, was "destroyed" as the innovation of digital streaming services became the norm. In this example, many people point to *Netflix* as the culprit responsible for closing their local video rental store; yet it was that very same *Netflix* that stated out as a company that rented out DVDs (on a mail-subscription basis).

So creative destruction, while bound to happen, really does open opportunities that did not previously exist. The key is being able to adjust, and to tailor your content and promotional efforts to those new opportunities. Self-reflection asks us to pause, step back and assess the "lay of the land"; to identify problems and embrace them. The goal of that practice is confirm that we are moving in the right direction.

CONTENT CREATION AND PROMOTION

Your most unhappy customers are your greatest source of learning.

Bill Gates Founder, Microsoft

STEVEN CHRISTIANSON

CHAPTER 15

ULTIMATELY, ...

In any company, regardless of size or structure (including self-employed, charities and non-profits), it is difficult to identify a function more important and pervasive as marketing. As David Packard, co-founder of Hewlett-Packard, once said, "marketing is too important to be left to be marketing department."

Marketing is about the very culture of the organization, its identity. Especially in the burgeoning world of digital reach, everyone is their own, or their organization's, "cheerleader". A 2017 article in the *New York Times* described marketing as "the art of telling stories so enthralling that people lose track of their wallets."

Marketing is actually so many things. It is often a mix of advertising and promotion, sales, communications, public and media relations, social media, branding, organizational culture, and research. We have discussed the perspectives of each of these components throughout this book. The terms "content creation" and "promotion" are used as the umbrella terms, but all of this activity falls within the world traditionally described as marketing. Many people distance the concept and practice of marketing from what they do; implying that marketing is something that only a small group of people or a department are engaged in. The fact is, everyone is involved in their company's content creation and promotion; they are, therefore, part of the marketing mix.

It is for this reason that budgets and efforts dedicated to marketing, or content creation and promotion, should not diminish during times of challenging cash flow. A knee-jerk reaction in moments of austerity points to the "marketing budget", believing that a reduction in efforts to tell your story and let people know you exist will somehow improve the bottom line. In fact, during those times when cash flow is weaker, it is often the case that more money and effort ought to be dedicated to content creation and promotion. At the very least, such moments should provide opportunity to determine if there are more effective methods to tell your story, to re-evaluate timing or distribution of effort.

You may be part of a political campaign. Perhaps you are a co-owner of an online or bricks-and-mortar retail store. You might work in the front office of a sports team. Perhaps you hold a managerial position in a church administration. You might work as a bank teller. In each of these examples, regardless of where your position is located in the organization's hierarchy, you are part of content creation and promotion: every time you speak to other employees or members of the team; every time you attend a conference; every time you speak with or meet your customers, voters, members or subscribers. Content creation and promotion are what you do, and constitute the critical components of what builds and maintains corporate culture or organizational identity.

In summation, let's consider some key take-aways.

Ultimately, …

1. Personalize your presence

Since the early days of marketing and communication, companies realized it was more effective to reach customers through a personal touch. Lovely women and cool guys sold cars. Animated characters sold hamburgers. Celebrities sold everything from beer to food products. And an English lizard is the most popular pitchman today for life insurance. Remember, personalize your presence

It's not just an endorsement; it's about giving

your message a face and personality. Maybe that personality is you, because it doesn't always have to be third-party spokesperson. As was pointed out in earlier sections, there is a reason why real estate agents plaster their mug shots on their lawn signs and professional profile cards. This is true whether you're a corporate company, a not-for-profit association, a political party or even if you're promoting your own services as a self-employed person. Give it a personality.

2. **Focus in on a main message.**

Too many people make the mistake of wanting to tell too many stories in a short amount of time and space. Remember – if people take one thing away from seeing your post, your ad, your animated graphic, or even your website, what do you want them to remember? Because there is only one thing they will remember – and that is usually only after multiple attempts at telling your story. If you want your listeners, readers or viewers to do something, make sure that it's easy and takes practically no time at all. A radio ad asking listeners to remember a phone number, slogan, company name, hashtag and website is not only too much information for the listener, it requires someone to somehow transcribe all that information (if they can remember it); not exactly easy for someone to do if that radio ad were listened to while driving a car.

3. Don't over-complicate things.

If you can't encapsulate your idea into the space of a lapel button, it's too complicated. More importantly, if you can't crystalize your thoughts into three, four or five words, then you probably are still a little fuzzy about the idea yourself.

4. Use every list of contacts you've got.

Grow your presence first with your existing contacts and networks. Introduce things through email to everyone you know. And ask each of them to do something specific and simple, like sharing your original message with three of their contacts. It all starts somewhere. Like the insurance sales associate we discussed in an earlier section, that person needs to think of at least 100 names of people that he or she knows. Those names are the preliminary leads for outreach, potential sales or recruitment. They are also the names that probably already reside within the category of trust, that place where your voice already has a level of influence and authority. Word-of-mouth is as important today as it ever has been.

5. Get to know where you do well with you messaging -- and where you don't.

While you may start out by coordinating your messaging on multiple social media channels simultaneously, you'll likely to do better on some more than others. Maintain a constant monitor on metrics every time you communicate something. Just because one of your products or projects received good response through one platform doesn't mean that level of success will be matched in another. Learn how and where you're engaging peoples' interest, and build on that potential.

6. Your medium also tells your story.

You probably wouldn't try to explain the details of a *PowerPoint* presentation over the radio or through a podcast; this type of story is better suited to a visual medium, like *YouTube*, for example. Similarly, using a book to teach a music student how to play a new piece is probably not as effective as using an app or website that combines the printed word with video and audio samples. Identifying the most suitable medium can augment your content by facilitating an enhanced potential for peoples' retention of your message. You'll ultimately hit their senses of sight and sound at the same time. This is particularly important for messages, projects or services that are more complicated and might need that extra teaching tool. So your choice of medium not only facilitates your message, but becomes part of the message itself.

Marketing's job is never done. It's about perpetual motion. We must continue to innovate every day.

Beth Comstock,
Former CEO and
Vice-Chair, GE

CHAPTER 16

LOOKING AHEAD

Harvard University scholar, Ronald Heifetz, has published and taught extensively on the principle of exercising leadership, particularly the practice of adaptive leadership. Within that body of work, Heifetz explores a key method of dealing with change, challenge and how to move forward, something he calls "getting on the balcony". In order to gain perspective in the midst of action, one ideally wants to develop the skill of getting off the "dance floor" and going to the "balcony". It's a mental activity of stepping back in the midst of action and asking ourselves, "what is really going on here?" As we look ahead, by stepping back and standing on the balcony, what emerges? What possible issues might we be confronting?

Amidst the rapid-fire changes going on

around us today, coupled with the uncertainties associated with the current pandemic (not to mention as-yet unidentified future economic and social disruptors), we can, nonetheless, anticipate several issues gaining prominence as we look ahead. Standing from the balcony, let's consider the following issues that could impact content creation and promotion, whether positively or negatively:

Privacy concerns are being addressed through legislative measures around the world. The Europe Union, Australia, the UK, much of South America, Canada, the United States, significant parts of Africa, the Asia-Pacific region, Russia and Mexico have enacted, or are in the process of enacting, legislative measures dealing with data and privacy concerns. Such measures affect how a company collects and uses information, including cloud storage, search engines and promotional activity in the digital world.

Accessibility issues are gaining prominence globally. In this context, accessibility refers to how usable something is for anyone with mobility issues, anyone living with a disability, as well as seniors. The needs of a user who has weakened or zero eyesight will be quite different that the person with 20/20 vision. A user without use of his or her hands would undoubtedly find text-to-speech and other audible applications quite beneficial. Users or customers for whom accessibility is critical represent a significant percentage of the overall population. According to UN estimates, those with disabilities and seniors, namely those for whom accessibility is critical, constitute upwards of 22% globally (that's the number, roughly speaking, in most Western countries; some global-south and lower-income countries might be higher). Furthermore, medical advances and healthier lifestyles are contributing to longer lifespans. In other words, a condition or disease that would have once ended someone's life at a relatively young age can now live a much longer number of years. This, coupled with the aging trend of many societies, suggests that this is a demographic group that demands attention. Telling your story, and knowing how to promote your content, to this demographic group suggests some initial challenges, but significant opportunities as well.

Mobile dominance will continue. More and more people will eventuate to predominantly mobile usage. As we discussed in earlier sections, China is overwhelmingly at this point already. But the switch in Western counties is advancing a rapid pace. If you're not optimized for mobile, this should be a primary focus.

The trend of corporate rebranding and the changing of monikers show no immediate signs of slowing. What some refer to as the "cancel culture", this momentum is a sort of digital shaming. And, make no mistake, it is very real. Easily mobilized, anything today can be a target for boycott, shaming or simply being canceled. Corporate and political leaders are especially sensitive to this activity. As we discussed earlier, there will emerge some opportunity associated with this trend, with some companies embarking on long-overdue re-brands.

Gaming today is more than online gambling and electronic games. The audience of e-sports and virtual competitive gaming is estimated at around 495 million people. This audience is expected to grow substantially. Platforms like Twitch have shown to be early leaders in the field. The world of gaming suggests impressive opportunity for anyone in the world of content creation and promotion.

Zero click-through results are becoming more common. These occur when a search engine company, let's say *Google*, provides results that are sufficiently adequate such that the user doesn't have to click through to another site. Zero click-through practices keep the user on the primary site where he or she conducted the search query, with a zero percentage of users clicking through to the websites returned in their results. Close to one-third of mobile users never click through on their search results. The implications for promotional effectiveness are considerable.

Internet networks always require more speed and greater reach around the world. These two insatiable requisites of digital access are currently being addressed through something broader than 5G: satellite internet service. Both *Amazon* and SpaceX are working to build space-based internet networks, called Kuiper and Starlink respectively. The plans entail launching thousands of satellites into orbit. Both companies then plan to offer subscription-based internet access anywhere around the globe. As of February 2021, SpaceX boasted more than 10,000 users of its Beta service. Greater access, higher speeds, a truly global reach of users and customers – this is a trend worth watching.

Podcasts actually find their origin in the 1980s, although they didn't really experience any degree of popularity until 2004-2005. There seemed to be a healthy potential around that time, then their popularity tapered off. Until recent years, that is. Podcasts can now be live; they can offer audio-only or video-included content. There are dozens of companies that produce, distribute or catalog podcasts. Celebrities are increasingly turning to the podcast as a means of content creation, and influencers are readily found in any podcast listing. Podcast revenue is currently estimated at $1 billion annually – a figure that should pique the interest of anyone working in content creation and promotion.

Virtual events have become the norm during the coronavirus pandemic. Shutdowns, lockdowns and social distancing put the fire of real potential under the notion of virtual events. Today, any given conference or meeting of international attendees is held virtually. While the restrictions and social behaviours associated with the pandemic will recede in the coming months and years, the cost effectiveness of virtual events will not.

Social media companies will increasingly offer self-publishing tools for content creators. Content is what everything is about, and existing social media giants know this. These efforts are part of a roll-out to keep content creators within a company's sphere of influence. For *Facebook*, the efforts are designed to assist writers to create subscription-based businesses. *Facebook* announced such measures in March 2021. *Amazon*, through its *KDP* services, has been upending the self-publishing industry for quite some time. Now, *Facebook* aims to help content creators to reach their audiences and receive payment for their content and promotional efforts. The company will offer a free, customizable publishing tool that will allow users to develop websites, email newsletters, and, most importantly, charge for subscriptions. A full suite of metrics will be available to the content creator to monitor activity and measure results. Similarly, *Twitter* announced plans to offer a subscription option for content creators. Not to be left out, *Snapchat*, *TikTok* and *Instagram* have also indicated that they plan to pay content creators, thereby bolstering the content on their platforms and reinforcing the foundations of the creators within their respective spheres of influence.

So, standing from the "balcony" does not help us predict the future or what the "hit song" will be; but it certainly allows us the opportunity to see just a little further down the road. The challenges and opportunities identified by looking ahead will define who is an innovator and who is a follower, who is a leader and who chooses to use last year's methods because they worked well at that time.

Everything around us is always in constant motion, so dedicate as much effort and as many resources to innovating your content and forms of promotion on a daily basis. The job of content creation and promotion is always a job in progress.

TAKE-AWAYS, QUESTIONS AND ANSWERS

QUESTIONS AND ANWERS

What is content creation and promotion?

This is a form of marketing, and, in fact, many people will refer to these activities as part of the marketing world. However, content creation and promotion focuses first on the customer and his or her needs. Traditional marketing focuses first on the company, its products and services – a very top down approach.

Is the content created free to the customer?

Quite often it is. Company blogs and podcasts typically don't require any payment; and many other types of content, like political content, usually doesn't ask a fee from voters. That said, if all products and services were viewed as content, we would likely see a far greater degree of customer-oriented interaction. So some content is fee-driven, but there is something that brings in the customer and establishes a connection prior to the dispensing of any fee.

What else may be described as content?

In addition to blogs or podcasts, content can also include how-to videos, written articles, online musical jam session, webinars and live forums. Content is just about anything in this context.

How do I approach putting together a plan to create effective content and promote that material?

Understand who you're talking to or whom you want to reach. Why do you want that profile of customer as opposed to another? And, ultimately, what do you want them to do. Whether it's about identifying votes, selling a bulk order of t-shirts, or getting someone to subscribe to a curated music stream, you first have to tackle these questions.

My team and I learned of a group that raised awareness of their cause by securing several thousand signatures as an expression of support. Can't I simply follow this path?

In a sense, you don't always need new content. The book you are about to publish can be promoted by using one of its sections as a focus of discussion in your blog or podcast. So it is possible to re-deploy existing content. However, replicating a plan and trajectory that was successful at another time is not a recipe for success.

Isn't social media simply a fad?

Social media is the very essence of moving content promotion to its next level: social commerce. While certain platforms or apps in the world of social media won't thrive indefinitely, social media as a transmitter is not likely going to diminish in importance. Social media is making profound effects on the stock market, on company brands, or corporate social positioning, and on the very nature of commercial transactions.

How do I keep on top of all the different social media, especially knowing that they differ by demographics? How do I know when are the most effective times to post, publish or engage?

Traditional marketing deployed content through multiple channels, in varying regions characterized by differing sensitivities. It's not all that different with social media. Scheduling ahead of time can be done with various tools and apps designed to diarize your content and promotional windows. This is a far easier approach than waking up at 2 am to post content on *TikTok*.

Metrics are so critical today. How can I get metrics on these activities and how will I know what works and what doesn't?

First, remember that we're dealing with the art of content creation and promotion. It is not a science, nor should it be treated as such. The ultimate aim in your efforts is human, so ensure that every step along the way reflects the quirks and nuances of this reality. Second, measurement is important, and is easily gleaned from the analytics in many apps and platforms. Like traditional forms of marketing, say putting an advertisement in a hard-copy newspaper, don't expect immediate results. The process entails perseverance, persistence and sometimes even a degree of repetition.

SOCIAL MEDIA TAKE-AWAYS

Facebook

Facebook is an American online social media and social networking service that was launched in 2004.

Facebook can be accessed from devices with Internet connectivity, such as personal computers, tablets and smartphones. After registering, users can create a profile revealing information about themselves. They can post text, photos and multimedia which is shared with any other users that have agreed to be their "friend", or, with a different privacy setting, with any reader. Users can also use various embedded apps, join common-interest groups, buy and sell items or services on *Marketplace*, and receive notifications of their *Facebook* friends' activities and activities of *Facebook* pages they follow. *Facebook* claimed that it had 2.80 billion monthly active users as of December 2020, and it was the most downloaded mobile app of the 2010s globally. (Source of Image and copy: *Wikipedia*)

Bottom Line

Facebook can be highly useful for sharing any content that is featured by an image. It is particularly good for helping introduce users to something, which, in this forum, typically requires that extra, targeted push – paid placement. While it can result in action, its main benefit is helping people know you are there. *Facebook* is also effective for building networks within the network by joining or creating groups. There is also a growing social commerce component to *Facebook*. Keep in mind that the demographic on *Facebook* is somewhat older than it used to be in its early days; correspondingly, the younger demographics of Generation Z and the Millennials tend to converge more heavily in other platforms. Content-heavy material won't find a robust audience on *Facebook*. The word "face" in the name is used for a reason.

When is the best time to post on *Facebook*?

Typically, especially for business pages, schedule your posts between 1 pm and 4 pm, while trying to avoid Tuesdays. Mid-afternoon on Sundays generate the highest level of engagement.

Twitter

Twitter is an American microblogging and social networking service, launched in 2006, on which users post and interact with messages known as "tweets". Registered users can post, like and retweet tweets, but unregistered users can only read them. Users access *Twitter* through its website interface or its mobile-device application software ("app"), though the service could also be accessed via SMS before April 2020. *Twitter*, Inc. is based in San Francisco, California, and has more than 25 offices around the world. Tweets were originally restricted to 140 characters, but was doubled to 280 in 2017. Audio and video tweets remain limited to 140 seconds for most accounts. By 2012, more than 100 million users posted 340 million tweets a day, and the service handled an average of 1.6 billion search queries per day. In 2013, it was one of the ten most-visited websites and has been described as "the SMS of the Internet". As of Q1 2019, *Twitter* had more than 330 million monthly active users. (Source of Image and copy: *Wikipedia*)

Bottom Line

Twitter is an excellent place to find reporters looking for breaking news. While many people post opinions and thoughts, *Twitter* is an effective vehicle to share useful information and articles about a topic, targeting a specific reporter you know covers and writes about such content. This can also generate a certain amount of attention on you and what you're doing, provided what you're sharing is constructive and useful.

When is the best time to post on *Twitter*?

From 12 noon to 1 pm. There are many apps and tools that help organize your posts, and these are best scheduled just prior to that 12 noon to 1 pm timeframe, the traditional break for lunch. Weekdays tend to receive a higher volume of activity, with Wednesdays in particular generating significant engagement.

Instagram

Instagram (commonly abbreviated to IG or Insta) is an American photo and video sharing and social networking service owned by *Facebook*, and was launched in 2010. The app allows users to upload media that can be edited with filters and organized by hashtags and geographical tagging. Posts can be shared publicly or with pre-approved followers. Users can browse other users' content by tags and locations and view trending content. Users can like photos and follow other users to add their content to a feed. *Instagram* was originally distinguished by only allowing content to be framed in a square. The service also added messaging features, the ability to include multiple images or videos in a single post, and a Stories feature – which allows users to post photos and videos to a sequential feed, with each post accessible by others for 24 hours each. As of January 2019, the Stories feature is used by 500 million users daily. After its launch in 2010, *Instagram* rapidly gained popularity, with one million registered users in two months, 10 million in a year, and 1 billion as of June 2018. *Instagram* became the 4th most downloaded mobile app of the 2010s. (Source of image and copy: *Wikipedia*)

Bottom Line

Instagram has really evolved into a useful platform for small businesses, restaurants and cafes, and group feeds for sports teams, music groups and tv shows. This is image-based, using video, Gif and still imagery. Want to promote your newest menu item or the film showing on a certain streaming network? *Instagram* is ideal for this type of content promotion, incorporating the ability to feature a Gif of the film or a photo of the meal. Easy for sharing and complete with hashtags, *Instagram* is perfect for that one-a-day dose of content from your team.

When is the best time to post on *Instagram*?

Saturday at 5 pm is a great time to schedule a post. That said, you'll find effectiveness by posting on Monday, Wednesday and Thursday either between 11 am and 1 pm or 7 pm and 9 pm. Most recent data show that the highest volume of user engagement is Wednesday.

Pinterest

Pinterest is an American image sharing and social media service designed to enable saving and discovery of information (specifically "ideas") on the internet using images and, on a smaller scale, animated GIFs and videos, in the form of pinboards. The site had over 400 million monthly active users as of August 2020. It is operated by *Pinterest*, Inc., based in San Francisco, and was launched in 2009. The creators behind *Pinterest* summarized the service as a "catalogue of ideas" that inspires users to "go out and do that thing", although that it is not an image-based "social network. It also has a very large fashion profile. *Pinterest* has also been described as a "visual search engine". *Pinterest* consists mainly of "pins" and "boards". A pin is an image that has been linked from a website or uploaded. Pins saved from one user's board can be saved to someone else's board, a process known as "repinning". Boards are collections of pins dedicated to a theme such as quotations, travel, or weddings. Boards with multiple ideas can have different sections that further contain multiple pins. Users can follow and unfollow other users as well as boards, which would fill the "home feed". In August 2016, *Pinterest* launched a video player that lets users and brands upload and store clips of any length straight to the site. In October 2013, *Pinterest* began displaying advertisements in the form of "Promoted Pins". Promoted Pins are based on an individual user's interests, things done on *Pinterest*, or a result of visiting an advertiser's site or app. In 2015, *Pinterest* implemented a feature that allows users to search with images instead of words. In March 2020, *Pinterest* introduced the "Today" tab on the home feed which shows trending pins. In 2017, *Pinterest* introduced a "visual search" function that allows users to search for elements in images (existing pins, existing parts of a photo, or new photos) and guide users to suggested similar content within *Pinterest*'s database. The platform has drawn businesses, especially retailers, to create pages aimed at promoting their companies online as a "virtual storefront". In June 2015, *Pinterest* unveiled "buyable pins" that allows users to purchase things directly from *Pinterest*. In March 2019, *Pinterest* added product catalogs and personalized shopping recommendations with the "more from [brand]" option, showcasing a range of product Pins from the same business. In 2020, there were over 335 million monthly active users with 88 million within the US. (Source of image and copy: *Wikipedia*)

Bottom Line

Pinterest embraces the idiom, "a picture is worth a thousand words". You don't have to be stuck with finding pretty or provocative images. A pie chart, graph or other info-graphic can serve the purpose here. Pins and shares are common on *Pinterest*. The realm of *Pinterest* originally was predominantly female. Today, the gender gap of users has closed considerably. Although it still is the go-to place for cooking-related content, a simple topic search will yield a broad spectrum of interests.

When is the best time to post on *Pinterest*?

Posting during the evenings tends to work best, between 8 pm and 11 pm, with Saturdays standing out. Avoid standard work hours during which to schedule a post. Although the gender gap has closed considerably, mothers tend to represent a highly active demographic.

Reddit

Reddit is a social news aggregation, web content rating, and discussion website.

Registered members submit content to the site such as links, text posts, and images, which are then voted up or down by other members. Posts are organized by subject into user-created boards called "communities" or "subReddits", which cover a variety of topics such as news, politics, science, movies, video games, music, books, sports, fitness, cooking, pets, and image-sharing. Submissions with more up-votes appear towards the top of their subreddit and, if they receive enough up-votes, ultimately on the site's front page. As of February 2021, *Reddit* ranks as the 18th-most-visited website in the world and 7th most-visited website in the US.. About 42-49.3% of its user base comes from the United States, followed by the United Kingdom at 7.9-8.2% and Canada at 5.2-7.8%. *Reddit* was founded in 2005. In February 2019, a $300 million funding round led by Tencent brought the company's valuation to $3 billion. The content is user-generated—including photos, videos, links, and text-based posts—and discussions of this content in what is essentially a bulletin board system. The name "*Reddit*" is a play-on- words with the phrase "read it", i.e., "I read it on *Reddit*." As a network of communities, *Reddit*'s core content consists of posts from its users. In addition to commenting and voting, registered users can also create their own subreddit on a topic of their choosing.

Bottom Line

Reddit has the advantage of user pages, groups and sub-groups. Ad placement can be targeted in very specific ways. Custom content can be easily posted and shared. If you engage and activate your existing networks, *Reddit* can really open up potential: like a hub of mini clubs, each with their own little websites (so to speak), you'll find just about everything there, but take the time to become familiar with membership rules, as well those for posting, ranking by Karma, and user engagement. *Reddit* certainly has immense potential, but many have attested to its unique quirks and nuances.

When is the best time to post on *Reddit*?

Early mornings. Saturdays, Sundays and Mondays, between 6am and 9am, is when most Redditors are most engaged.

TikTok

TikTok, known in China as *Douyin*, is a video-sharing social networking service owned by Chinese company *ByteDance*. The social media platform is used to make a variety of short-form videos, from genres like dance, comedy, and education, that have a duration from three seconds to one minute (three minutes for some users). *TikTok* is an international version of *Douyin*, which was originally released in the Chinese market in September 2016. Later, *TikTok* was launched in 2017 in most markets outside of mainland China; however, it only became available worldwide after merging with another Chinese social media service, Musical.ly, on August 2, 2018. *TikTok* and *Douyin* have almost the same user interface but no access to each other's content. Their servers are each based in the market where the respective app is available. The two products are similar, but features are not identical. *Douyin* includes an in-video search feature that can search by people's face for more videos of them and other features such as buying, booking hotels and making geotagged reviews. Since its launch in 2016, *TikTok/Douyin* rapidly gained popularity in East Asia, South Asia, Southeast Asia, the United States, Turkey, Russia, and other parts of the world. As of October 2020, *TikTok* surpassed over 2 billion mobile downloads worldwide. The *TikTok* mobile app allows users to create a short video of themselves. The "For You" page on *TikTok* is a feed of videos that are recommended to users based on their activity on the app. Content is generated by *TikTok*'s artificial intelligence (AI) depending on the content a user liked, interacted with, or searched. Users can also choose to add to favorites or select "not interested" on videos for their page. *TikTok* combines the user's enjoyed content to provide videos that they would also enjoy. Users and their content can only be featured on the "for you" page if they are 16 or over as per *TikTok* policy. Users under 16 will not show up under the "for you" page, the sounds page, or under any hashtags.

The app's "react" feature allows users to film their reaction to a specific video, over which it is placed in a small window that is movable around the screen. Influencers often use the "live" feature. This feature is only available for those who have at least 1,000 followers and are over 16 years old. If over 18, the user's followers can send virtual "gifts" that can be later exchanged for money. One of the newest features as of 2020 is the "Virtual Items" of "Small Gestures" feature. This is based on China's big practice of social gifting. Since this feature was added, many beauty companies and brands created a *TikTok* account to participate and advertise this feature. With quarantine in the United States, social gifting has grown in popularity. As the platform has grown significantly over the past few years, it has allowed companies to advertise and rapidly reach their intended demographic through influencer marketing. The platform's AI algorithm also contributes to the influencer marketing potential, as it picks out content according to the user's preference. Sponsored content is not as prevalent on the platform as it is on other social media apps, but brands and influencers still can make as much as they would if not more in comparison to other platforms. Influencers on the platform who earn money through engagement, such as likes and comments, are referred to as "meme machines". (Source of image and copy: *Wikipedia*)

Bottom Line

TikTok is fun, but the capacity to spread a short clip among several thousand people in a couple of minutes is very real. This network caters to custom content that is easily sharable. Eighty-five percent of businesses already use video as a marketing tool. The primary user demographic on *TikTok* is notably younger, so video content that is humorous or features animals constitutes the lion's share of content. This platform is young in another way: it was launched in Western markets only in 2018. Influencers tend to reside here in larger numbers, so one form of promotion attractive to many at this point is paid promotion by an influencer. Pay attention to your user demographics on this platform. For example, you might be able to spread the message about your political candidate rather effectively, but the users in the network might be too young to vote.

When is the best time to post on *TikTok*?

The answer to this one really does vary. It kind of depends on who you are, what type of content you're promoting, and where you want to promote it. That said, there are metrics that show when user engagement is high: Tuesdays at 9 am; Thursdays at 12 noon; and Fridays at 5 am. While the times shown here are EST, keep in mind that users are global, so a little time-zone arithmetic is required sometimes. Also, pay close attention to analytics in the app, which will provide account holders with a decent overview of usage, engagement and other demographic-related information.

LinkedIn

LinkedIn is an American business and employment-oriented online service that operates via websites and mobile apps. Launched in 2003, the platform is mainly used for professional networking, and allows job seekers to post their CVs and employers to post jobs. As of 2015, most of the company's revenue came from selling access to information about is members to recruiters and sales professionals. Since 2016, it has been a wholly owned subsidiary of Microsoft. As of December 2020, *LinkedIn* had 760 million registered members from 150 countries. *LinkedIn* allows members (both workers and employers) to create profiles and "connect" to each other in an online social network which may represent real-world professional relationships. Members can invite anyone (whether an existing member or not) to become a "connection". Users can obtain introductions to the connections of connections (termed *second-degree connections*) and connections of second-degree connections (termed *third-degree connections*). In mid-2008, *LinkedIn* launched

LinkedIn DirectAds as a form of sponsored advertising. In October 2008, *LinkedIn* revealed plans to open its social network of 30 million professionals globally as a potential sample for business-to-business research. It is testing a potential social network revenue model – research that to some appears more promising than advertising. In 2013, *LinkedIn* announced their *Sponsored Updates* ad service. Individuals and companies can now pay a fee to have *LinkedIn* sponsor their content and spread it to their user base. This is a common way for social media sites such as *LinkedIn* to generate revenue. The goal is to create a comprehensive digital map of the world economy and the connections within it. (Source of image and copy: *Wikipedia*)

Bottom Line

LinkedIn used to be described as the professional's version of *Facebook*. If the aim of promotion is you, this network can be very effective. Getting a job, or recruiting a candidate, has become one of the strengths of *LinkedIn*. This is also a forum with company- and professionally- oriented content. People are not typically sharing family or vacation photos on *LinkedIn*. However, let's say you wanted to promote a new home office innovation, this network may be right for you. Again, as with most networks, offer something useful, something of value to the users. Don't just blurt out "here's my product or service ... now buy it."

When is the best time to post on *LinkedIn*?

Mid-morning during the middle of the week. Tuesdays, Wednesdays and Thursdays show the best results, typically from 10 am to 11 am.

YouTube

YouTube is an American online video-sharing platform headquartered in San Bruno, California. The service, created in February 2005, was bought by *Google* in November 2006 for US$1.65 billion and now operates as one of the company's subsidiaries. *YouTube* is the second most-visited website after *Google Search*. *YouTube* allows users to upload, view, rate, share, add to playlists, report, comment on videos, and subscribe to other users. Available content includes video clips, TV show clips, music videos, short and documentary films, audio recordings, movie trailers, live streams, video blogging, short original videos and educational videos. Most content is generated and uploaded by individuals, but media corporations including *CBS*, the *BBC*, *Vevo*, and *Hulu*, offer some of their material via *YouTube* as part of the *YouTube* partnership program. Unregistered users can watch, but not upload, videos on the site, while registered users can upload an unlimited number of videos and add comments. As of May 2019, there were more than 500 hours of content uploaded to *YouTube* each minute and one billion hours of content being watched on *YouTube* every day. *YouTube* and selected creators earn advertising revenue from *Google AdSense*, a program that targets ads according to site content and audience. The vast majority of videos are free to view, but there are exceptions, including subscription-based premium channels, film rentals, as well as *YouTube Music* and *YouTube Premium*, subscription services respectively offering premium and ad-free music streaming, and ad-free access to all content, including exclusive content commissioned from notable personalities. Based on reported quarterly advertising revenue, *YouTube* is estimated to have US$15 billion in annual revenues.

In 2018, *YouTube* started testing a new feature initially called "*YouTube* Reels". It was later renamed "*YouTube* Stories". It is only available to creators who have more than 10,000 subscribers and can only be posted/seen in the *YouTube* mobile app. Both private individuals and large production companies have used *YouTube* to grow audiences. Independent content creators have built grassroots followings numbering in the thousands at very little cost or effort. *YouTube*'s revenue-sharing "Partner Program" made it possible to earn a substantial living as a video producer – its top five hundred partners each earning more than $100,000 annually and its ten highest-earning channels grossing from $2.5 million to $12 million. By early 2013

Billboard had announced that it was factoring *YouTube* streaming data into calculation of the *Billboard Hot* 100 and related genre charts. (Source of image and copy: *Wikipedia*)

Bottom Line

YouTube is primarily known as a visual medium (although it has a rich and growing volume of audio-only content). As such, depending on your product or service, it can be useful for reviews, demonstrations, how-to's, lessons, conference content, and short docu-content. Ad placement on *YouTube*, as with many other online properties and apps, is also an excellent tool for spreading and reinforcing awareness. But it's the original content you upload, or that which is created by influencers to talk about your product, cause or service, that can help give momentum to the views and shares.

When is the best time to post on *YouTube*?

Just prior to the timeframes during which people will tend to watch anything. Viewers generally browse video content during the evenings, so make sure your content is up and ready by that time. The best time to post is between 12 noon and 4 pm, typically on Thursdays and Fridays. Heavy traffic occurs on weekends.

Snapchat

Snapchat was initially released in 2011. Revenue in 2019 was estimated at $1.7 billion USD. *Snapchat* primarily used for creating multimedia messages referred to as "snaps"; snaps can consist of a photo or a short video, and can be edited to include filters and effects, text captions, and drawings. Snaps can be directed privately to selected contacts, or to a semi-public "Story" or a public "Story" called "Our Story." The ability to send video snaps was added as a feature option in December 2012. By holding down on the photo button while inside the app, a video of up to ten seconds in length can be captured. After a single viewing, the video disappears by default. On May 1, 2014, the ability to communicate via video chat was added. Direct messaging features were also included in the update, allowing users to send ephemeral text messages to friends and family while saving any needed information by clicking on it. Friends can be added via usernames and phone contacts, using customizable "Snapcodes," or through the "Add Nearby" function, which scans for users near their location who are also in the Add Nearby menu. In November 2014, *Snapchat* introduced "Snapcash," a feature that lets users send and receive money to each other through private messaging. The payments system is powered by Square. The *Wall Street Journal* reported in May 2017 that *Snap Inc.*, the company developing *Snapchat*, had signed deals with NBCUniversal, A&E Networks, BBC, ABC, Metro-Goldwyn-Mayer, and other content producers to develop original shows for viewing through *Snapchat*'s "Stories" format. According to the report, *Snap* hoped to have several new shows available on a daily basis, with each show lasting between three and five minutes, and the company has sent out detailed reports to its partners on how to produce content for *Snapchat*. Over 2017 and 2018, *Snap* and partners launched several shows. In June 2020, *Snapchat* announced the creation of its first-ever "shoppable" original show: "The Drop," focused on "exclusive streetwear collabs" from celebrities and designers. Viewers will learn about the item for sale and how it came together as well as what time that day the item will go up for sale. (Source of image and copy: *Wikipedia*)

Bottom Line

Snapchat is image-based and focuses on a decidedly younger demographic, primarily Gen Z age-group. The biggest use for *Snapchat* tends to be comedic content, such as animated faces. There is a large audience here. A key point of advice focuses on knowing who you want to reach, ensuring that your content is not only suitable for a younger age-group, but speaks to this audience in a meaningful way.

When is the best time to post on *Snapchat*?

Any day of the week tends to work equally well. Higher levels of user engagement occur in the evening, particularly later at night. The best times to post show promise after 10 pm. Any day of the week really works. But for increased engagement post later at night.

Anchor

Anchor is a free platform for podcast creation. It contains tools that allow users to record and edit audio, arrange it into podcast episodes, publish podcasts to listening platforms, and monetize content by collecting listener contributions or adding advertisements into episodes. The recordings need not be professionally produced or edited and no expensive equipment is required. Beginners often start out using nothing more than their smartphones. The app includes a library to store user recordings, royalty-free music, as well as sound effects available to all users. *Anchor* can be used on *iOS, Android, iPad* and web browsers. The company first launched as a social audio service geared for short-form content. In February 2018, *Anchor* launched an updated version of the platform specifically for creating and publishing podcasts. In February 2019 *Anchor* was acquired by *Spotify* and operates as a subdivision of the streaming company. (Source of image and copy: *Wikipedia*)

Bottom Line

Anchor is a podcast creation and distribution platform. Your podcast episodes can be as frequent as your wish. Although length really isn't an issue, a good pod is not more than 10 minutes (and even half of that is better). Every company, every person, has something to say. *Anchor* lets you record and upload. *Anchor* then publishes to a wide range of streaming apps. Some companies use this content to augment (even replace) the corporate blog. Elected officials have been known to host weekly outreach and town-hall programs that feature interviews with owners of local businesses, student athletes, seniors ... you name it. The podcasts are easily shared and tagged. For the elected official, the podcast helps reinforce brand and profile in the community, positioning the politician as a listener, one who asks questions, one highlights the importance of people, and one who embraces new ideas and innovation –essential qualities when considering the re-electability (or saleability) of a candidate.

When is the best time to publish on *Anchor*?

Schedule your publishing times for 2 am either Wednesday or Thursday. Although significant distribution is immediate, it is best to allow some time for a fuller distribution to take effect.

Thursdays, throughout the pm timeframe, show higher levels of listens and downloads. Like many of these platforms, *Anchor* provides analytics and very good information about listening patterns.

GLOSSARY

Accessibility
This refers to all aspects that influence a person's ability to function within an environment. Accessibility affects the design of products, devices, services, as well as operating environments for anyone living with mobility restrictions, including seniors, or other types of disabilities.

App
This is the abbreviation for application. An app is a piece of software that can come pre-installed on a device or as software that is downloadable for self-installation. Apps typically run locally on your device, but can also run through a web browser.

Artificial Intelligence (AI)
This is the simulation of human intelligence in machines that is programmed to think or operate like humans, thereby mimicking human actions. The term is also applied to any machine that exhibits traits associated with the human mind, such as learning or problem-solving.

Cancel Culture
This is a contemporary form of ostracism that expels someone (living or historic) from social or professional reference. The practice often manifests through the withdrawal of support for

public figures or companies (thus the cancelling effect), typically when a social media-based movement identifies an action that the public figure or company has either referenced or made that is deemed offensive.

Click-through
A click-through is the action of following a hypertext link to a particular website, especially a commercial one. The action of
clicking through often opens a new page or website, thereby taking the user from the originating page or site.

E-Commerce
Electronic commerce, or e-commerce, is a business model that lets businesses and individuals buy and sell things over the Internet.

Platform
A platform in the computing world typically refers to a computer's operating system. It is a set of software and a surrounding ecosystem of resources. A platform enables growth through connection. The value of a platform derives not only from its own features, but from its ability to connect external tools, teams, data, and processes.

Podcast
A podcast is an episodic series of (usually) spoken word digital audio files that a user can

download to a personal device. Streaming applications and podcasting services help integrate and manage a user's personal consumption queue across many podcast sources and playback devices.

Posting
This refers to the act of publishing or sharing something on social media.

Social Commerce
Distinct from e-commerce, social commerce is the process of selling products or services directly on social media. The entire shopping and transaction experience – from product discovery, research, comparisons, check-out processes and payment – takes place on a social media platform and within the social media experience.

Social Media
Social media are interactive digitally-mediated technologies, such as websites and apps. These facilitate the creation or sharing/exchange of information, expression and ideas through virtual communities and networks.

Soundmark
This is usually a short distinctive melody or sequence of sound that is used to perform the trademark function of uniquely identifying the commercial origin of a product or service.

Related terms include sound trademark, audio logo, sonic logo and sound logo.

Spam/Anti-Spam
Spam is any kind of unwanted, unsolicited digital communication, (email or text message), that is distributed in bulk. Spam is also referred to as junk mail. Anti-spam is any type of remedy that may include software and filters, regulations and laws.

Trademark
This is a type of intellectual property that consists of a recognizable sign, design, or expression that identifies a product or service, or source of those products or services, as being distinct from others.

Visual Identifier
This visual identifier is tangible (unlike a brand, which is intangible). It is the visual representation, that which you can see. Ideally, branding and visual identity (through visual identifiers) are harmonized. Sometimes a visual identifier can evolve separately from the brand, and thereby become a more potent and lasting image in the customer's (or audience's) perception.

FURTHER READING

Barnum, P.T. *Barnum's Own Story: The Autobiography of P.T. Barnum.* New York: Dover Publications, 2017.

Bezos, Jeff. *Invent & Wander: The Collected Writings of Jeff Bezos.* Brighton, MA: Harvard Business Review Press, 2020.

Champion, Justin. *Inbound Content: A Step-by-Step Guide To Doing Content Marketing the Inbound Way.* Hoboken: Wiley, 2018.

Charvet, Shelle Rose. *Words that Change Minds: The 14 Patterns for Mastering the Language of Influence.* Hamilton, ON: Institute for Influence, 2019.

Davis, Dorothy. *A History of Shopping.* London: Routeledge and Kegan Paul, 1966.

Diehl, Gregory V. *Brand Identity Breakthrough: How to Craft Your Company's Unique Story to Make Your Products Irresistible.* Buffalo, Wyoming: Identity Publications, 2016.

Gil, Carlos. *The End of Marketing: Humanizing Your Brand in the Age of Social Media and AI.* London: Kogan Page, 2019.

Hall, Kindra. *Stories that Stick: How Storytelling Can*

Capture Customers, Influence Audiences, and Transform Your Business. New York: Harper Collins Leadership, 2019.

Handley, Ann. *Everybody Writes: Your Go-To Guide to Creating Ridiculously Good Content.* Hoboken: Wiley, 2014.

Hanly, Laura. *Content That Converts: How To Build A Profitable and Predictable B2B Content Marketing Strategy.* Self-published, CreateSpace Independent Publishing Platform, 2016.

Heifetz, Ronald A., Marty Linsky and Alexander Grashow. *Practice of Adaptive Leadership: Tools and Tactics for Changing Your Organization and the World.* Brighton, Massachusetts: Harvard Business Review Press, 2009.

Higgins, Denis, Ed. *The Art of Writing Advertising: Conversations with Masters of the Craft.* New York: McGraw-Hill, 2003.

Huffington, Arianna. *Thrive: The Third Metric to Redefining Success and creating a Life of Well-Being, Wisdom, and Wonder.* Easton, PA: Harmony, 2015.

Johnson, Matt and Prince Ghuman. *Blindsight: The (Mostly) Hidden Ways Marketing Reshapes Our Brains.* Dallas: BenBella Books, 2020.

Lock, Andrew. *Walt Disney's Way: How to Build a Better Business Using the Magical Marketing Strategies of Walt Disney: 17 Success Secrets for Entrepreneurs.* Henderson, NV: Addictive Publications.com LLC, 2020.

Lund, Kevin. *Conversation Marketing: How to Be Relevant and Engage Your Customer by Speaking Human.* Newburyport, MA: Weiser, 2018.

Norris, Dan. *Content Machine: Use Content Marketing to Build a 7-Figure Business With Zero Advertising.* Self-published, CreateSpace Independent Publishing Platform, 2015.

Pulizzi, Joe. *Epic Content Marketing: How to Tell a Different Story, Break through the Clutter, and Win More Customers by Marketing Less.* New York: McGraw-Hill Education, 2013.

Schaefer, Mark W. *The Content Code: 6 Essential Strategies to Ignite Your Content, Your Marketing, and Your Business.* Self-published, 2015.

Schnoor, Aaron. "The Secret of Disney's Brand: How the Company has become a Marketing Empire." *Better Marketing*, March 17, 2020.

Sheridan, Marcus. *They Ask, You Answer: A Revolutionary Approach to Inbound Sales, Content Marketing, and Today's Digital Consumer.* Hoboken: Wiley, 2019.

Sutherland, Rory. Alchemy: *The Dark Art and Curious Science of Creating Magic in Brands, Business and Life*. New York: William Morrow, 2019.

Turner, Gavin. *Content Marketing: Proven Strategies to Attract an Engaged Audience Online with Great content and Social Media to Win More Customers, Build Your Brand and Boost Your Business*. Self-published, 2019.

Wilson, Pamela. *Master Content Strategy: How to Maximize Your Reach & Boost Your Bottom Line Every Time You Hit Publish*. Nashville: BIG Brand Books, 2018.

INDEX

A

accessibility.. 172, 212
adaptive leadership 171
Amazon . 53, 175, 176
Anchor 130, 148, 149, 209, 210, 211
anti-spam laws 40
apps .36, 40, 133, 136, 148, 158, 180, 181, 182, 186, 198, 200, 205, 210, 212, 214
artificial intelligence (AI)........... 197, 212
audio logo. 10, 18, 95, 97, 99, 215
authority and influence 50, 51, 52, 117, 156

B

Barnum, P.T....10, 68, 69, 70, 71, 115, 116, 126, 158
bricks-and-mortar .. 8, 106, 154, 165

C

Cancel Culture 60, 212
China (market development) . 107, 108, 109, 110, 154, 173, 196, 198
click-through 174, 213
commercial jingle . 85, 86, 95, 97
creative destruction 159, 160

D

digital currency 155

E

e-commerce 8, 10, 106, 153, 154, 213, 214
e-integration 105, 106, 107, 110
e-sports 174

F

Facebook.. 38, 39, 71, 103, 130, 134, 135,

142, 146, 176, 182, 183, 184, 187, 201

G

Google 19, 21, 174, 203
government 37, 48, 50, 76, 77, 78, 80, 88, 97

I

Instagram 106, 130, 146, 147, 176, 187, 188

L

LinkedIn 43, 130, 142, 143, 200, 201, 202

M

metrics 145, 157, 168, 176, 181, 199
military 17, 59
moniker 10, 48, 49, 55, 56, 58, 60, 80, 173
moving advertisement 80
music ... 10, 83, 85, 86, 87, 88, 89, 90, 91, 95, 96, 97, 146, 168, 179, 188, 193, 203, 209

P

persuasion 88, 123, 126, 127, 130, 150
Pinterest 130, 140, 141, 190, 192
podcast ... 71, 99, 100, 148, 168, 175, 178, 179, 209, 210, 213
power .. 11, 26, 30, 50, 78, 80, 89, 110, 117, 119, 120
privacy 6, 40, 172, 182
promotion 11
public persona 5

R

re-branding 56
Reddit   71, 116, 130, 138, 139, 156, 193, 194

S

Snapchat 106, 176, 206, 208
social causes 9, 40, 46, 47, 50, 51, 70

social commerce... 10, 103, 105, 106, 107, 109, 110, 111, 115, 134, 154, 180, 183, 214
social media..... 10, 36, 39, 40, 60, 71, 105, 106, 116, 121, 129, 150, 154, 155, 158, 164, 167, 176, 180, 182, 190, 196, 198, 201, 213, 214
social positioning.... 9, 45, 47, 48, 50, 51, 55, 56, 180
sound trademark .. 95, 215
soundmark 10, 18, 95, 96, 97, 98, 99, 100, 214
spam 119, 215
sponsorship 46, 48, 49

sports teams 10, 60, 146, 188

T

TikTok 106, 130, 144, 145, 176, 181, 196, 198, 199
trust ... 5, 11, 109, 110, 115, 116, 117, 119, 121, 122, 128, 167
Twitter .. 71, 130, 132, 133, 176, 185, 186

V

visual identifiers.... 10, 75, 76, 77, 78, 80, 215

Y

YouTube 100, 106, 130, 136, 137, 144, 168, 203, 204, 205

Continue reading to learn more about the

Explained! Series

Henley Point Productions

ABOUT EXPLAINED!

The *Explained!* series was born from a need to find compact, conversational and instructive material that was up-to-date, comprehensive and readily available to just about anyone.

This first book in the series, *Content Creation and Promotion*, was originally released in February 2021. It was initially inspired by a young entrepreneur who had asked the question, "How do I get my brand out there?" From that simple inspiration, *Content Creation and Promotion* was written in an attempt to explain how to enhance brand position, organizational personality and overall image, which have become universally important in creating and promoting content. The lessons learned in this book extend beyond traditional product and service marketing, and apply equally to advocacy and social causes, election campaigns and even differentiation of charity organizations. As the book cover conveys, *Content Creation and Promotion* explains why and how you can reach -- and retain -- your desired audience.

Podcasting was identified as the second work, related to content creation and promotion, but providing the reader with a perspective from *behind the microphone.*

The series of *Explained!* Books also aims to

provide the reader with a concise presentation of each topic that is comprehensive enough to serve as a reference guide, compact enough for the busy reader, conversational to a degree that technical terms and topics many people shy away from (like speaking to large audiences or putting your creative ideas there) are rendered more relatable, yet sufficiently authoritative and instructive that the reader truly walks away with a new skill – or, at least, a new perspective.

COMING SOON TO A GLOBAL MARKETPLACE NEAR YOU

Steven Christianson's newest book,

Podcasting – Explained!

Release Date: Spring 2021

Sneak Preview from *Podcasting - Explained!*

Chapter 2

IT ALL STARTED WITH A MICROPHONE

Actually, it all started with the Greeks (or so some say). The ancient Greeks were known for many contributions to western civilization. Among them were the use of public forums and amphitheatres for a variety of purposes, including speeches, debates, theatre, and oratory. But once a lot of people assemble into a single forum or amphitheatre, one quickly discovers the need to increase the volume of one's voice. They dealt with this issue in 5th century BC Greece by developing theatre masks with horn-shaped mouth openings that amplified the voice of the actor using the mask. It ended up looking like a customized megaphone. Essentially, it was a microphone

ABOUT THE AUTHOR

Steven Christianson has a life-long career in content creation and promotion. A public policy analyst by vocation, he has nearly 30 years of executive success in government relations, parliamentary engagement, advocacy and issues promotion. He runs a Toronto based firm that specializes in content development and promotion. He spent many years building an international GR portfolio at a major non-profit. Steven previously worked with the Parliament of Canada, with a focus on policy development and communication. His early career began as a research director for the Royal Commission on Aboriginal Peoples. He also gained valuable insights for five years as a Delegate to the Council on Economic and Social Development at the United Nations.

Steven lives in Toronto with his wife and two cats.

Visit
StevenChristianson.ca
for more information.

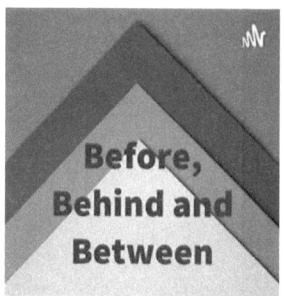

The official podcast of Steven Christianson is located at

https://beforebehindandbetween.wordpress.com